Learning About Language & Literacy in Preschool

From the editors of *Teaching Young Children*

Learning About
Language & Literacy
in Preschool

From the editors of *Teaching Young Children*

National Association for the Education of Young Children
Washington, DC

National Association for the Education
of Young Children

NAEYC Publishing

Chief Publishing Officer
Derry Koralek

Editor-in-Chief
Kathy Charner

Managing Editor
Mary Jaffe

Senior Editor
Holly Bohart

Senior Graphic Designer
Malini Dominey

Designer
Victoria Moy

Associate Editor
Meghan Dombrink-Green

Associate Editor
Elizabeth Wegner

Assistant Editor
Lauren Baker

Editorial Assistant
Ryan Smith

Through its publications program, the National Association for the Education of
Young Children (NAEYC) provides a forum for discussion of major issues and ideas
in the early childhood field, with the hope of provoking thought and promoting
professional growth. The views expressed or implied in this book are not necessarily
those of the Association or its members.

Permissions
The box on pages 70–71 is adapted with permission from Nell R. Carvell, Language
Enrichment Activities Program (LEAP), vol. 1 (Dallas, TX: Southern Methodist Uni-
versity, 2006).

Credits
Cover design: Edwin C. Malstrom
Photographs: Copyright © Tyler Hamlet: 99 (top); Judy Jablon: 74; Lisa Mufson
Koeppel v (bottom), 14–16, 100 (top), 101; Sandra Lighter-Jones: 53 (bottom), 91;
NAEYC: cover (right), 9, 33, 35, 37, 61, 77 (top and bottom), 83; Marilyn Nolt: 57, 62
(left), 87 (right and left), 88; Karen Phillips: 8 (left), 11, 40 (left), 75, 99 (bottom right);
Karen B. Pratt: 89; Michael Rosen: 68, 98 (top); Shari Schmidt: vii (bottom right), 8
(right), 12, 69; Ellen B. Senisi: cover (left and center), v (top), vii (left and top right), 4,
5, 6, 17, 32, 52, 54 (left), 55, 60, 62 (right), 63, 72, 86, 98 (bottom); Thinkstock: 34; Susan
Woog Wagner: 39, 53 (top), 54 (right)
Courtesy of article authors: vi (bottom left and top right), 30–31, 38, 40 (right), 41,
42–45, 48, 78–81, 97
Courtesy of Carroll County (Maryland) Public Library: 51 (top and bottom),
99 (bottom left)
Courtesy of Baltimore County Public Library: vi (bottom right), 49, 50, 51 (top), 100
(bottom)
Illustrations: Copyright © Jennifer O'Connell: 18–25; NAEYC: 66–67

Library of Congress Control Number: 2014945390
ISBN: 978-1-938113-10-9
Item 7227

CONTENTS

Introduction

Meghan Dombrink-Green

The Very Hungry _____

Brown Bear, Brown Bear, _____?

_____ and the Terrible, Horrible, No Good, Very Bad Day

Goodnight _____

Don't Let the _____ Drive the _____!

Do you recognize the books above? Of course you do! It doesn't matter that there are some words missing from the titles. You know these titles, and you know these books. Not only that, you probably have a favorite among them, know if one of them is in rotation in your classroom library, and could quote a few pages for anyone who asked. Like I said, you *know* these books.

Think about that for a minute. You recognize these titles—or phrases—even when there are words missing. You can fill in the blanks because you are familiar with the language and have read these books tens—maybe hundreds—of times. Can the preschoolers in your program identify these book titles? Can they extend the book and tell you what *they* see? They probably can. Why? Because of the repetition of the words, because they are familiar with language, and because of a love of books that you have shared with them.

Before he could read, my nephew Sean could recite page after page of his favorite books. He loved to connect book passages with what he saw around him, often stopping to point out how standing on a tree stump was like his favorite character at the park. Once he walked down the street with his dad and insisted on stopping to hug a tree because it was what a character in a book did. While this has made for long walks on short city blocks, Sean's love of books has led to a varied vocabulary. He adores the words *precarious* and *suspect*. He confidently uses new—and long—words to describe what is in his younger sister's hair or explain why he would not like to eat the broccoli on his plate.

Young children love to play with language, and they have a natural inclination to do so (Yopp & Yopp 2009). Alliteration, rhyming, or a carefully chosen "wrong" word can send children into giggles. When preschoolers extend the word play and insert their own ideas, they demonstrate a finer understanding of words, syllables, and sounds.

Educators can use books in a variety of ways to build children's knowledge and love of literature. They can also offer books that will inspire and comfort children during challenging times. As Sue Mankiw and Janis Strasser explain in "Using Read-Alouds to Explore Tender Topics" (see p. 86), books can help children understand their own experiences and relate to their peers.

About This Book

In this book you will find strategies that help children extend their language and literacy learning. Read about how to use show-and-tell to build children's confidence in speaking in front of others (p. 30). Explore how real-life experiences inspire children to write (p. 38). Think about how creating and learning raps can help children's oral language skills (p. 60).

The tips for supporting dual language learners describe ways to help children who are learning two or more languages at the same time. These tips were written by Karen N. Nemeth, author of *Basics of Supporting Dual Language Learners* (NAEYC, 2012).

The Reflective Questions help you think about yourself as a teacher and about the specific children

in your program. The Thinking Lens®, which is a way of examining your teaching practice, comes from Deb Curtis and colleagues at Harvest Resources Associates, LLC.

As you start reading this book, remember these words from poet David McCord, "Books fall open/you fall in." Fall into this book and explore new places and ideas that will inspire and engage you.

REFERENCE

Yopp, H.K., & R.H. Yopp. 2009. "Phonological Awareness Is Child's Play!" *Young Children* 64 (1): 12–21.

Language & Literacy

Reading, Writing, and Talking: Strategies for Preschool Classrooms

Kathleen A. Roskos, James F. Christie, and Donald J. Richgels

R eading, writing, listening, and talking are all parts of early literacy learning—and they're all connected. It's important for young children to learn to understand spoken language, become aware of the different sounds in language, and start learning about printed letters and words. Preschoolers need writing to help them learn about reading and reading to help them learn about writing. They need to talk and listen to help them learn about both.

Preschoolers learn about literacy through the everyday things they do in your classroom. It's especially important to encourage a love of reading and to demonstrate the power of writing to communicate ideas. When you say, "Bilal, please help me hold the book and turn the pages," you teach children about handling books and the left-to-right, top-to-bottom orientation of English. When you guide children's small hands and eyes to printed words on the page, this shows them that marks have meaning. When you listen to children "read" their scribbles, you encourage them to assign meaning to the marks they have made.

How else can you encourage preschoolers to love reading, writing, and oral language so much that they're positively stampeding to the literacy center? The following strategies are a great start.

Literacy Teaching Strategies

There are countless ways to encourage children's love of reading, writing, speaking, and listening. Here are nine of the best. As you read them, think about how many of these ideas can be worked into children's play.

1. **Hold meaningful, thought-provoking conversations.**

   When talking with children,
   - Listen and respond to their questions and comments
   - Use unusual words, such as *colander* and *loft*
   - Expand what children say, offering more description and using grammatically mature language (If a child says, "It runned out," you might respond, "Your marker ran out of ink!")
   - Challenge children to imagine, remember, and think about things they see and hear around them
   - Invite children to play with sounds and words and think about spoken language itself

2. **Read aloud to individual children and groups.**

   Begin with a collection of diverse, high-quality children's books. Then be sure to
   - Read aloud to the class at least once every day
   - Share a variety of stories, poems, and information books over time

   - Talk to children about the text before, during, and after reading
   - Offer activities related to the books read aloud
   - Read favorites again and again
   - Read aloud books that reflect children's cultures and languages
   - Read aloud to one or several children as often as you can

3. **Explore the sounds of language to increase phono-logical awareness.**

   Children love to play with sounds and words, and often find this quite funny. Play games and listen to stories, poems, and songs that involve
   - *Rhyme*—have fun with words that end with the same sound ("See you later, alligator")
   - *Alliteration*—play with words that begin with the same sound ("The *r*acecar *r*aced . . . into the *r*estaurant")

- *Sound matching*—play games to find which word begins with a specific sound ("Listen to the word *duck*. Duck starts with the /d/ sound. Which of these words starts with the same sound as duck: bird, dog, or cat?")

4. **Include alphabet activities.**

Offer materials to help children learn the letters of the alphabet, including

- ABC books
- Magnetic letters
- Alphabet blocks and puzzles
- Alphabet charts

It helps to connect letter names to meaningful things for children, such as their names ("Look, the names Jennifer and Jamal both start with *J*").

5. **Support emergent readers as they try to read books and other forms of print.**

Young children need times and spaces to explore books and print on their own or with friends. You can help them by

- Creating a well-designed literacy center stocked with lots of good books, props for inventing and retelling stories, and writing materials
- Rereading favorite books, especially predictable books with which children can chime in
- Filling the room with meaningful print, such as daily schedules, helper charts, labels that show where materials are stored, reminders ("Pump the soap 1 time")
- Encouraging print in play, such as providing menus for a pretend restaurant or suggesting children create them

6. **Provide books in the literacy center, in other areas of the room, and outdoors.**

Be sure to offer a wide variety of styles and topics, such as

- Information books and magazines which introduce new vocabulary and concepts
- Books, songs, and poems with strong rhymes, for example Raffi's *Down by the Bay*
- Stories with strong narrative plots, such as *Sophie's Squash* by Pat Zietlow Miller
- Books in children's home languages and in English
- Books that reflect children's cultures, families, and life experiences
- Classic and new literature
- Books with beautiful, inspiring illustrations

7. Support emergent writing.

Young children need easy access to materials so they can build their writing skills, including scribble writing, random letter strings, and invented spelling. Offer them

- A writing center (perhaps part of the literacy center) stocked with pens, pencils, markers, paper, and book-making supplies
- Demonstrations of writing (for example, listen to and write down a child's description of her drawing)
- Opportunities for meaningful writing—center sign-up sheets, library book checkout slips, Please Save! signs for unfinished block buildings or puzzles, charts that summarize a shared experience
- Writing materials children can use in their play (for example, pencils and notepads to write prescriptions, take orders, or create grocery lists)

8. Explain how books and print work.

While introducing and reading books or other texts, help children learn the conventions of print by

- Pointing to the print as you read it
- Inviting children to notice the differences between pictures and print
- Showing how books in English are read from left to right, top to bottom
- Pointing out different parts of books, like the cover and the title page
- Encouraging children to join in with repeated lines when you read their favorite stories

9. Offer activities that explore a topic.

When children choose and then study a topic, such as shoes or pizza, they gain valuable background knowledge and have opportunities to use reading, writing, and language skills. Children can

- Listen to the teacher read topic-related information from books, websites, or other sources and look at these resources on their own
- Gather data using observation, experiments, interviews, and such
- Record observations and information
- Revisit what they have learned through dramatic play

Above all, make sure children enjoy and succeed in reading, writing, and spoken language experiences. When children have fun with literacy activities, they will come back to them again and again, creating healthy learning habits now and for years to come.

Many preschoolers are learning to

- Name and write alphabet letters
- Hear rhymes and sounds in words
- Recognize and write their own names
- Spell simple words
- Learn new words from stories, work, and play
- Listen to stories for meaning

Sagacious, Sophisticated, and Sedulous: Introducing 50-Cent Words to Preschoolers

Molly F. Collins

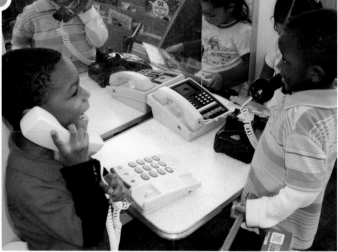

A teacher once told me, "Don't use a 50-cent word when a 5-cent word will do."

Well-meaning adults, including preschool teachers, often do this when they use simple words instead of complex words when talking with young children. Perhaps they think that preschoolers won't be able to understand sophisticated vocabulary. Complex words are high level, communicate details, and are less common in our everyday language. But, teachers can boost the knowledge of soon-to-be readers by introducing, using, and explaining the meaning of *sophisticated vocabulary*.

Early Language Foundations

Typically children learn vocabulary through conversations with adults. Preschoolers who hear rich explanations of sophisticated words learn many more words than children who do not (Collins 2010). It takes longer for children with limited vocabularies to learn new words. Understanding word meanings is a very important part of reading comprehension. Therefore, children with limited vocabularies tend to have a more difficult time grasping what they read.

Benefits of Introducing 50-Cent Words

Discussing words with children encourages them to be thinkers and problem solvers. Read-aloud times are great opportunities to talk about rare words. The teachers in the following examples engage children in conversations about words found in the story.

1. Introduce new words and concepts.

Ms. Doran introduces the word *unruly* while discussing *Henry's Happy Birthday*, by Holly Keller.

Ms. Doran: *Unruly* means hard to control. It was hard for Henry to make his hair stay down. Your hair might be unruly when you wake up in the morning.

Jason: Yeah, my mom's hair is messy.

Ms. Doran: When she wakes up?

Jason: Yeah, all over, like this (hands circling head).

Ms. Doran: It sounds like her hair is unruly, like Henry's hair. It is hard to control.

Ms. Doran's use of *unruly* while speaking about Henry's appearance exposes children to a sophisticated word whose concept they can easily understand.

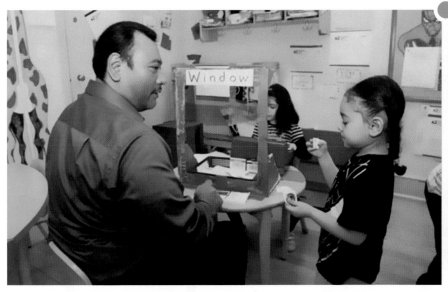

2. **Clarify differences in meaning between words that are new to the children and concepts they already know.**

Mr. Myers reads aloud Lindsay Barrett George's *In the Woods: Who's Been Here?* In talking with the children he points out slight differences in the meaning of words. He provides general information to help the children understand a sophisticated vocabulary word, *splay*.

Mr. Myers: When it (pointing to butterfly) was inside, its wings were together, but once it got out, it could *splay*, or spread out, its wings.

Aquala: Yeah!

Mr. Myers: *Splay* means to spread out.

Aquala: Yeah, like peanut butter. Spread with a knife.

Mr. Myers: But the peanut butter doesn't really get splayed because it doesn't have parts. Splay means to spread something that has parts. You have body parts that you can splay. Your arms and legs can spread out like this (gestures).

Aquala: (pointing to stomach) Can't splay this!

Mr. Myers: No, you can't splay your stomach or your tongue. You can only splay things that have parts to spread out.

Aquala: (spreading arms apart) Is this splay?

Mr. Myers: Yes, you are splaying your arms.

When Aquala applied a literal understanding of *spread*, Mr. Myers knew he needed to clarify. He explained that splaying requires parts (like body parts) and differs from spreading a substance (like peanut butter).

3. **Help children deepen their understanding of words.**

Ms. Fradon reads aloud William T. George's *Box Turtle at Long Pond*. She uses a group discussion to help Garth develop a deeper understanding of the word *predator*.

Ms. Fradon: A *predator* is an animal that eats other animals.

Garth: Like a tiger. A tiger eats an antelope.

Ms. Fradon: Yes.

Garth: Because (pointing to raccoon) they eat turtles.

Ms. Fradon: So, a raccoon is a predator of?

Garth: Of the ... (pointing to turtle)

Ms. Fradon: Box turtle. Exactly.

Caritina: (pointing to raccoon) Yep, that's a predator.

Garth has some knowledge of predators through examples (he knows that tigers are predators). Ms. Fradon's definition of the word *predator* helped him fully understand the meaning. He showed this understanding by saying that a raccoon is a predator because it eats turtles.

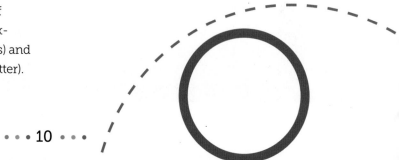

4. Use conversations to clarify initial misunderstandings.

Sometimes children miss important distinctions in the meaning of a word. They might not hear the word precisely or could misapply their existing knowledge about language. A teacher-led conversation can help to ensure everyone understands the word's meaning. Mr. Chua and the children discuss illustrations of bunting during a reading of *Henry's Happy Birthday*.

Mr. Chua: Do you know what bunting is?

Antoine: Uh-uh [no].

Mr. Chua: (to Val) Do you know?

Val: Uh-huh [yes]. It's putting up things.

Mr. Chua: That's almost right. Bunting is a decoration.

Val: Uh-huh.

Mr. Chua: It's cloth or paper that is hung up at parties. It is a decoration—something pretty. Sometimes grown-ups put bunting up to decorate a room or the outside of a building.

Because the word *bunting* ends in -ing (like *throwing* or *riding*) Val thinks that it involves action. Mr. Chua clarifies that bunting is something that is put up, not the action of hanging something.

Implications for Teaching

Teaching sophisticated vocabulary requires that adults know the words and their variations. In addition, teachers must model thinking outside the book.

Knowing What to Know

Children first need to know the typical, common definition of a word. Knowing a word includes under-

standing how its meaning can vary, depending on how it is used. When teachers use the same word in different scenarios, it strengthens children's understandings of the word's meaning. An umbrella's fabric *repels* water. Bug spray *repels* insects. Although these ideas differ, both mean to "push away from" or "ward off."

Exposure to the same word across settings can also teach differences in meaning. A shirt can have *crisp*

folds. *Crisp* crackers break easily. Morning air can feel *crisp*. Knowing words means learning variations. This requires early, continued exposure across contexts.

Thinking Outside the Book

Throughout the day, teachers can use words already introduced in books. This encourages children to use the words in their own conversations.

- Use sophisticated vocabulary deliberately with children throughout the day. This provides repeated exposure and helps children understand what the word means in different contexts. For example, a teacher might explain the word *persevere* when it is first encountered in a storybook. Later she uses it during activities with children and then uses it again during a conversation.
- Provide concrete examples of sophisticated vocabulary. For example, when washing berries, show and label a sieve. Define *sieve*—a wire mesh utensil—and explain its function: in this case, draining water from washed fruit. Show examples of types of sieves, discuss different functions (for example, sifting, puréeing), or show examples of sieves in different contexts, such as construction or archaeology. Invite children to use sieves in cooking and in outdoor and water play activities.

Children need opportunities to practice new vocabulary in different settings. Small groups are especially helpful for dual language learners and children who tend to be shy. In small groups children can use the word in an authentic way: "I am using the sieve to sift the flour." Children can compare new information to what they already know, offer additional new information themselves, and evaluate information shared by other group members.

A Few Parting Words

Teachers and families must be *sagacious* (wise) while exposing preschoolers to sophisticated words and helping children use them during conversations and activities. They must be *sophisticated* (complex) while choosing and talking about worthy words. Finally, we must be *sedulous* (diligent) in preparing to teach and use vocabulary during different activities and experiences. If young children develop large vocabularies, they are more likely to become strong readers who understand what they read. The 50-cent words are worth it.

REFERENCE

Collins, M.F. 2010. "ELL Preschoolers' English Vocabulary Acquisition From Storybook Reading." *Early Childhood Research Quarterly* 25 (1): 84–97.

Reflective Questions ?

Know Yourself
- Think of a time you heard a word or phrase that was new to you. How do you approach learning new words and meanings? What is your comfort level in playing with, learning, and using complex vocabulary?
- How would you assess your own vocabulary and your use of complex words with children? What would you need to do to increase your use of 50-cent words?

Consider Multiple Perspectives
- What beliefs and values underlie teachers' use of sophisticated vocabulary with young children? What learning outcomes might result from this?
- What other perspectives on the use of sophisticated vocabulary should be considered? How might cultural or family background influence ideas about complex vocabulary?

Examine the Environment
- Observe your physical setting. Identify places where the joy of sharing words happens often. What might you add to encourage more vocabulary?

Find the Details of Children's Competency
- Listen carefully to children as they play. Notice specific examples of children using complex vocabulary. Where can you observe individual children's strengths and competencies with language as they play?
- Notice children who use languages other than English. How can you encourage their use of sophisticated vocabulary?

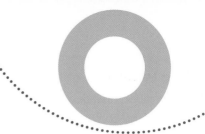

Supporting Writing in Preschool

Janis Strasser and Lisa Mufson Koeppel

Preschool children start to write long before they ever learn to read. Lisa, coauthor of this article and a preschool teacher, notes, "Teaching children to love writing and to understand its value and importance is one of the most important goals of a preschool program, even more important than getting them to form letters and words correctly."

It's center time in a class of 4-year-olds and seven of the children are writing as they play.

In the block center, Devon and Jonathan are taping a sign they have just completed onto their building. They tell the teacher that it says, "Firehouse. Don't be ascared of loud bells." She asks if they want to make up a name for their firehouse and write it on the sign.

In the art center, Cameron is making a birthday card for his daddy. He asks the teacher how to write "Happy Birthday." She suggests that he look at the birthday cards in the classroom greeting card collection.

In the dramatic play center, transformed into a pizzeria, Elaine is using a note pad to take food orders from Wany'ae and Amari. She "reads," "Pizza with meatballs and two pizzas with lots of cheese."

In the writing center, Shivani is choosing paper to staple together so she can write a book about her new puppy. She starts by drawing a picture of the dog.

Here are 10 ways to support writing and help children put their thoughts on paper.

1 Supply *every* center.

Include various types, shapes, colors, and sizes of paper, crayons, pencils, markers, tape, and scissors. Add new materials as the children's interests change.

2 Create a well-stocked writing center.

Have envelopes and stationery, magazines, pieces of wrapping paper, wallpaper samples, some teacher-made blank books, stickers, blank labels, and writing and drawing tools. Invite children to write or dictate stories, and suggest that they "read" their stories to their classmates. Encourage reluctant writers to dictate stories to you. You can also dictate stories for children to write down. This is especially exciting to children at the inventive spelling stage.

3 Value children's writing attempts.

Most children go through stages of emergent writing, from scribbles to letterlike forms and finally to real letters. It is important for a young child to see him- or herself as a writer/author whose marks on paper have meaning. Explain that no two people write the same way. Comment on children's efforts without placing too much emphasis on letter formation until they are ready.

4 Share children's writing.

Display it in the classroom, and send their writing home. Explain to families in newsletters, workshops, or notes accompanying their children's work that the children's writing attempts have real meaning.

Comment on children's writing.

5 As children "read" their writing to you, ask questions to support and expand their writing, like, "Can you describe what the puppy looks like?" or "Do you think you will remember who gets the pizza with meatballs, or do you need to write the names of your customers next to their orders?"

Model the value of writing.

6 Let children see you writing in a daily journal, making a list of supplies to order for the classroom, jotting down notes about them, and writing reminders to yourself. While you are writing, say, "I'm writing a note that says 'guitar' to stick on my door so I'll remember to bring it to school for music time tomorrow." Provide sticky notes so the children can write their own reminders.

Display various types of print.

7 Post print around the room, and integrate it into writing activities. Display words that have meaning to the children and that support their writing. Examples include lists of the children's names, phrases like "Happy Birthday" and "I Love You," street signs, labels for materials and interest areas, charts with words of favorite songs and poems, class rules, and so on. Plan activities that involve "reading the room." Tell the children that they will be explorers with clipboards and pencils. Have them hunt for certain letters, names, or words and then write them on their clipboards.

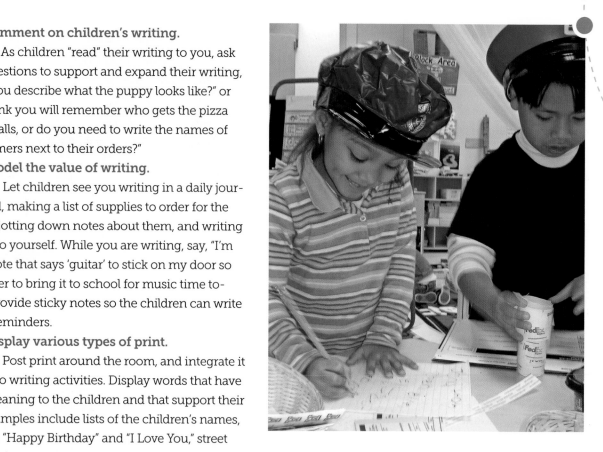

Collect items from real-life settings.

8 Whenever you visit a supermarket, bank, restaurant, medical office, store, or another everyday place, ask for literacy materials unique to that setting for children to use during play. These include order pads, menus, appointment cards, blank receipt pads, and so on. You will be amazed at how cooperative shopkeepers and business professionals are once you begin this quest! Also, send home a letter to families requesting similar materials.

Take a classroom writer's tour.

Every couple of weeks, notice whether you need to replace or refresh writing tools in each center. What can you add or change about your writing center, relative to the current interests of the children, to make it more inviting?

Consider each child's writing.

Observe child writers and collect samples of their work. Use what you know about particular children to plan exciting experiences and provide new materials to further enhance their writing!

Resource for Directors

Seplocha, H., J. Jablon, & J. Strasser. 2007. *The Essential Literacy Workshop Book: 10 Complete Early Childhood Training Modules.* Beltsville, MD: Gryphon House.

Resources for Teachers

Matteson, D.M., & D.K. Freeman. 2005. *Assessing and Teaching Beginning Writers: Every Picture Tells a Story.* Katonah, NY: Richard C. Owen.

Pinnell, G.S., & I. Fountas. 2011. *Literacy Beginnings: A Prekindergarten Handbook.* Portsmouth, NH: Heinemann.

Schickedanz, J.A., & R.M. Casbergue. 2009. *Writing in Preschool: Learning to Orchestrate Meaning and Marks.* 2nd ed. Newark, DE: International Reading Association.

Schickedanz, J.A., & M.F. Collins. 2013. *So Much More Than the ABCs: The Early Phases of Reading and Writing.* Washington, DC: NAEYC.

Literacy Learning Center

Laura J. Colker

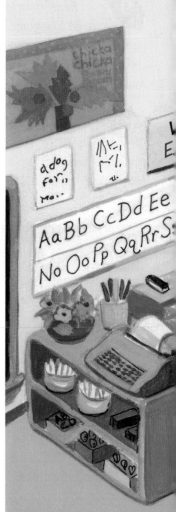

What Children Do and Learn

Language and Literacy

- Learn new words like *Parasaurolophus*.
- Play with the sounds of words or phrases like sheep tug and sheep shrug in the rhyming book *Sheep in a Jeep*, by Nancy E. Shaw.
- Learn letter names and that letters represent sounds and that words are made up of letters.
- Remember and understand stories by retelling them using puppets or flannel boards.
- Listen to and look at books with teachers to learn how print works.
- Sign their names to artwork, make signs for the block area, write home-made books and letters.

Math

- Count along in stories such as *The Baker's Dozen: A Counting Book,* by Dan Andreasen. Every time the baker makes another treat, children can count and wink along with him.
- Write or use stamps and ink pads to add page numbers to homemade books.
- Look at and discuss concept books.
- Put out materials for two children in front of two chairs at the writing table.

Social and Emotional

- Develop relationships with school staff and community members by drawing, dictating, or writing thank-you letters.
- Make "All About Me" books. Children can create and reread books on their favorite subject—themselves.
- Learn about people by reading about people who have different cultures, life experiences, or points of view.

Storytelling
Contar cuentos

Our visit to a small, small pond
We went to a pond like in the book. Marta saw a tadpole. Ramon saw a soda can in the water. We used a big stick to get it out.

Nuestra visita a un estanque muy muy chiquito
Fuimos a un estanque como el del libro. Marta vio un renacuajo. Ramón vio una lata en el agua. La sacamos con un palo muy largo.

Reading
Lectura

Setup Tips

- Select books that reflect children's interests, abilities, families, cultures, and languages.
- Offer new materials regularly to support current projects and children's evolving skills and interests.
- Arrange the space so children can work alone, with a friend or two, or in small groups.
- Leave an open space where children can gather for story time or another large group activity.

Budget Stretchers

- Use the school or community library.
- Get books from online booksellers, yard sales, secondhand stores, dollar stores, and outlets.
- Exchange books with other preschool classrooms.
- Ask home improvement stores for old wallpaper sample books. Children can write on the backs of samples or use them to line the covers of their homemade books.

Include Children's Families and Cultures

- Invite family members to volunteer to read aloud, write children's dictations, or go to the library with the class and help children pick out books.
- Prepare tip sheets on literacy topics such as choosing books, reading aloud, finding print all around us, modeling reading and writing, and using websites like PBS Kids Raising Readers (www.pbskids.org/read) and Colorín Colorado (www.colorincolorado.org).
- Provide a list of basic, inexpensive writing materials. Suggest ways to create a portable or permanent writing area where children can draw, scribble, and write at home.
- Share home literacy ideas in newsletters or emails. One idea: Prepare a shopping list with your child's help. Write items as they name them. At the store, have your child cross off the items as you find them.
- Encourage families to routinely go to the community library and participate in children's events there.
- Ask families to suggest books that are their children's favorites or that represent their culture or background to include in the classroom library.
- Request that parents record themselves reading storybooks or poems. Children can play these recordings when they want to hear their parents' voices.

Beyond the Basics

- Include a computer and printer (with power cords out of children's reach) so children can print and keep or display their creations. Children can also use the computer to visit literacy websites. A computer program or website will read the same story aloud 100 times without tiring.
- Provide adaptive computer devices for children with physical, visual, or hearing disabilities.

A Place for Publishing
Lugar para publicaciones

Printer Paper
Papel para la impresora

Digital Camera - Cámara digital

Magazines - Revistas

Paste
Pegamento

Scissors
Tijeras

Stapler
Engrampadoras

Hole Pu
Perforad

Cray
Crayo

My Bird
by Eli Cole

One day I
found a bird.

All About Me

by Antonia Ruano

Luis and Minka
Make a Race
Track

Our Field Trip to
the Fire Station

Mrs. Bond's Class

Francois
Crosses the
Monkey Bars

Our Families

Nuestras familias

A Place for Publishing

Laura J. Colker

A place for publishing, housed within the literacy center, offers the tools and space children need to write, illustrate, and produce books. They might write and publish books about events at home or at the program, meaningful accomplishments, field trips, and other topics of interest.

Materials—Paper, cardboard, scissors, tape, crayons, stapler and staples, brads, a hole punch, and yarn, string, or laces to bind the book; any other items that lend themselves to making books.

Book Publishing Steps

Tell a story: A child dictates a fiction or nonfiction text to a teacher who writes it on paper in the child's home language and English. Some children may create a wordless picture book, telling a story with illustrations only.

Illustrate the book: Children draw, paint, or cut pictures out of magazines; print pictures from websites; or take digital photos.

Create the pages: Children gather their completed pages—both text and illustrations.

Put it together: Make covers out of construction paper or cardboard. Print the title and author's name on the cover and the title page. Laminate covers. Bind books with staples or brads, or punch holes in the pages and covers, then thread yarn, string, or laces through the holes.

Enjoy the finished product: Teachers help children display and share their books with classmates. Children read the books alone, share them with friends, and take them home to read with their families. Teachers read the books aloud at group time.

Note: As an alternative, use a computer to publish books.

What Children Do and Learn

Math

- Recognize and repeat patterns while making page borders with stencils.
- Measure pages, covers, and yarn or laces.
- Understand the meaning of symbols while counting and numbering pages.

Social and Emotional

- Share materials.
- Take turns using the computer and other equipment.
- Self-regulate and cooperate while making and carrying out plans alone or with a friend.

Physical

- Move a mouse to select an image.
- Type on a keyboard.
- Cut with scissors.
- Use a hole punch.
- Draw and paint with a variety of tools.

Setup Tips

- Use a table large enough to hold equipment and provide space for children to work.
- Place table near outlets; wind plastic ties around cords to prevent tripping.
- Locate in an area of the literacy center away from children who are quietly reading books.

Include Children's Families and Cultures

- Invite parents to provide photos so the children can make books about their families.
- Ask families for help translating key words and phrases into children's home languages.
- Encourage families to donate magazines (in English and home languages) so children can cut out and use pictures as illustrations.

Budget Stretchers

- Look for used, but still useful, computers, printers/scanners, and digital cameras at yard sales, on Craigslist, and through the Freecycle Network, www.freecycle.org. Ask families and local businesses to donate used equipment.
- Apply for grants to cover the cost of equipment. For example, seek computer equipment through the US General Services Administration's Computers for Learning program (www.computersforlearning.gov).
- Accomplish the same goals without using technology. Children can gain literacy and related skills through low-tech book-making strategies.

Children's Book Authors on Reading

Meghan Dombrink-Green

 t a recent National Book Festival in Washington, DC, several children's book authors and illustrators suggested ways preschool teachers can use their books to support preschoolers' literacy.

The Lion and the Mouse, by Jerry Pinkney. 2009. Little, Brown.

This wordless 2010 Caldecott Medal winner illustrates an Aesop fable. A lion spares a mouse he was going to eat. When the lion later gets caught in a trap, the mouse returns the favor by helping to free him.

The Tortoise and the Hare, by Jerry Pinkney. 2013. Little Brown Books for Young Readers.

Slow and steady wins the race! This classic fable is told through Jerry Pinkney's detailed illustrations. Children will never tire of this book—noticing something new every time they look at the illustrations. After he loses the race the Hare is a great sport, placing the medal around Tortoise's neck after the race.

Tips From Jerry Pinkney

Invite children to tell the story by reading the pictures. "It would be an interesting thing for teachers if they had different children read the story and then compare how each read it."

Encourage conversations. "Ask what parts of the pictures they [children] find most interesting."

Help children notice details in the illustrations. A teacher might say, "Look at the bandannas worn by the Tortoise and the Hare." Pinkney says he uses small details in many of his stories to "try to engage young children to be curious."

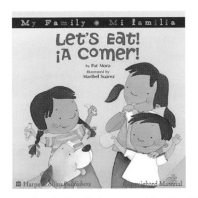

Let's Eat!/ ¡A comer!, by Pat Mora. Illus. by Maribel Suárez. 2008. HarperCollins.

"It's dinnertime. Look at all the food! /Es la hora de cenar. ¡Cuánta comida!" A Hispanic family prepares and eats dinner while showing gratitude for their blessings. Warm, colorful illustrations celebrate the family's close relationships and foods they eat. This book is the first in Mora's My Family/Mi familia bilingual series.

Bravo, Chico Canta! Bravo!, by Pat Mora and Libby Martinez. Illus. by Amelia Lau Carling. 2014. Groundwood.

The youngest of 12 mice in his family, Chico Canta lives in a theater. The mouse family likes to watch the plays and shout "Bravo!" along with the audience. Mrs. Canta speaks many languages and encourages her children to do the same.

Tips From Pat Mora

Select books that reflect diversity. "Children need to see themselves in books! We always say, 'Books are so important, books are so powerful.' If we believe that, then we have to showcase children in books."

Find volunteers to read books in children's home languages. "Be creative in partnering with someone in the school or a parent or an older child who can come in and co-read [in children's home languages]."

Support parents. "As professionals, the role we need to assume is literacy coach to parents of the children with whom we work."

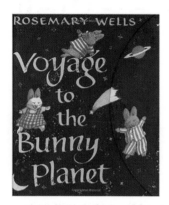

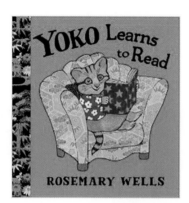

Voyage to the Bunny Planet, by Rosemary Wells. 2008. Viking.

This volume comprises a three-book set (*First Tomato*, *The Island Light*, and *Moss Pillows*). In each story, a small bunny has a terrible day. Things get better when Queen Janet whisks each bunny away to the magical Bunny Planet to experience "the day that should have been" before returning them to the real world.

Yoko Learns to Read, by Rosemary Wells. 2012. Hyperion.

Yoko is excited to learn how to read, and her mother is eager to help her. Since her mother only knows how to read in Japanese, Yoko worries that she will not be able to read English as well as the other children in her class. With love and support from Yoko's family, she learns to read through looking at pictures, sounding out letters, and recognizing words from the wall at school.

Tips From Rosemary Wells

Respect children's perspectives. "Both writing and reading are extremely private activities. And I always believe in respecting whatever the child is going to take away from my book."

Offer books in a series. "Children need structure, and they need repetition, and they need to feel safe. And nothing feels as safe as seeing characters again in a brand new book."

Make reading a positive, fun experience. "My message to teachers is simple: I try to create lovers of books. I don't like to have a lot of serious questioning going on about the book. I'd rather have it read again."

Shared Reading Can Help Preschoolers Build Literacy Skills

Laura J. Colker

S hared reading in preschool uses oversize books with large print and predictable text.

After reading the book at least once to enjoy the characters and story, the teacher places the book on an easel so everyone can see the illustrations and text. The children listen as she reads and talks about features of the text. Researchers have found it an effective way to introduce children to the joys of reading and enhance their print awareness (Grabmeier 2012).

To use shared reading with preschoolers,

- Present the title: "The name of this book is The Very Hungry Caterpillar. I'll point to each word in the title as I say it. On the cover, you can see what this hungry caterpillar looks like."
- Introduce the author and illustrator: "This is the name of the author, Eric Carle. He wrote all of the words in the story. He also created these brightly colored illustrations."
- Announce your reading plan: "I will be reading the text aloud. In this book it is on the left side, across from the illustrations."
- Explain where on the page you will be reading: "I'm going to read the words that go around the illustration. Watch my finger point to each word as I read it."
- Point out the words that characters speak before reading them: "Here's where the penguin speaks. I'm going to read his speech to the turtle now."
- Point out differences in print to children: "This *H* is an uppercase letter. See how it is bigger and different than these lowercase letters in black?"
- Ask questions about print as you read aloud: "What letter is this?" "Is there a letter in this word that's also in your name?"
- Point out print features: "This is the letter *P*. It starts words like *picnic* and *people*. Can you think of a word that begins with *P*?"

REFERENCE

Grabmeier, J. 2012. "Preschoolers' Reading Skills Benefit From One Modest Change by Teachers." Research and Innovation, Ohio State University. http://researchnews.osu.edu/archive/printrefer.htm.

Sharing Time: So Much More Than Show-and-Tell

Marie Sloane

The preschool class gathers expectantly around Andrew and Steven's block structure. "This is a jungle fury rocket," their teacher reads from the caption the boys dictated to her earlier in the day. They stand proudly beside their work. She continues, "The horse has a jumpy. The baby horse has a rocket. The horse has a rocket ship. The baby horse has a plane. The dad takes him on a ride if he wants to go to Las Vegas."

"Time for questions and comments," Andrew chimes in. "Umm, Jenna," he calls on a classmate who is raising her hand.

"I like the rocket," Jenna offers. After the teacher prompts her to ask a question to go with her comment, Jenna asks, "How did you make the jumpy?" Andrew explains a few of the things they put together to build it. Sharing time continues as Steven takes his turn to call on a classmate. The teacher winds things up with, "Thank you for sharing, Steven and Andrew. Let's move back to the green rug to see Karen's painting."

Why do this activity? Like show-and-tell, sharing time lets children practice speaking in front of a group, share something that is important to them, and build their language skills. During this time, children present work they are proud of and want others to see. It involves no toys or things brought from home. It is all about the children's learning, their ideas, and their accomplishments. The children share structures they build with blocks and reusable resources, pictures they paint, books they make, and their science center or outdoor discoveries. Almost anything can become a "share," as long as it is a child's high-quality work. No materials or preparation are needed.

What can children learn? Children who might hesitate to speak in front of a group are motivated to try. Cool ideas and discoveries are spread through the class. Children's learning and pride in their work are highlighted. Older children can write some or all of their own dictations. Families see some of the amazing things the children do each day that they might otherwise miss. Children glow with excitement and pleasure as others value their accomplishments.

Vocabulary words: Words will naturally present themselves as children in the group use words that other children do not know.

Lead Small Groups

1. During work time children build, paint, draw, create, or discover something they want to share with the rest of the class. (If a number of children want to share, create a sign-up list.)
2. Teachers check to see if the children's work is ready to be shared and encourage the children to expand and build on their ideas.
3. Children dictate a description of their work to a teacher, who writes down their words.
4. Children write their names (and the date, however they can) on the dictation.
5. Work to be shared remains in place at cleanup time. Children love this!
6. During group time everyone gathers around the work being shared. Teachers read children's dictations to the rest of the class. Classmates ask questions and comment on the work as the children who created it glow with pride!

Name(s): MADDY
Date: APRIL 2009

Tell us about your work:

THIS IS a SHIP People drive on the circle thing wheN It gets out of gas It gets gas this gas from Square

Respond to Individual Needs

Children who are reluctant to speak or learning English might participate at first as part of a group. As they learn what to do, they can be coached to present a solo share. It's important to support each child's home language, so enlist bilingual volunteers to take dictation or support a child sharing in her home language. English speakers will learn a little more of another language in the process.

Follow Up After the Activity

After children share a structure, painting, or discovery, it is ready to be taken home or cleaned up. Teachers print a photo of the children's work and glue it onto dictation forms. They send dictations home, post them as examples of the children's learning, or put them into the children's portfolios.

Involve Families

1. Send photos and dictations home with children to share with their families.
2. Suggest parents talk with their children about the sharing experience, their work and learning, and the products and discoveries shared by their classmates.

The Teacher's Role

As facilitators of the sharing process, teachers

- Help children who have never shared before get started
- Challenge children who like to share to do something new
- Encourage children to add counting, recognizing letters or numbers, or other academic skills to what they are doing
- Help children explain what they did and how, so the rest of the class can understand the process and the outcome
- Help children weave unrelated ideas together
- Celebrate children's hard work and achievements

Shoebox Stories

Carolyn Carlson

Why do this activity? Reading and other language skills go together. For a child to become a successful reader, he or she must understand the structure of language, know when and how to use it, and have a rich and growing vocabulary. Preschool teachers play an important role in helping young children develop and use language skills to express their ideas, build relationships with peers and adults, and talk about the things that interest them.

What can children learn? Children develop language skills while identifying objects, describing how the objects can fit into the story, and creating and sharing their stories. In addition, the children practice literacy skills by inventing characters, plot, and setting.

Vocabulary words: New words will naturally come up as children in the group use words that other children do not know.

Materials:
- A shoebox
- A random collection of items such as a spoon, a toy car, a stamp, a pair of sunglasses, a crayon, a ball, a key, and so on

Prepare for the Activity

1. Fill a shoebox with the random items collected to do the activity.
2. Clear a space for the children to work. This could be a table or a small space on the carpet. Children should have enough space to move around freely and should be able to hear each other when speaking.

Lead Small Groups

1. Invite four to six children to participate.
2. Introduce the box to the children and explain that it contains many different items—that don't seem related now. Explain to the children that together they will invent a story about those items. Teachers may want to read or provide an example for the children to look at to better understand what they'll be working on as a group. Or, teachers could introduce the activity by modeling the process during group time.
3. Open the box and invite children to explore the objects inside. They may want to describe the objects in the box and talk about how the objects are typically used.
4. Have the children begin to develop their stories. Teachers can ask questions to prompt these stories such as, "What would someone use this object for?" Or "How is _____ using the spoon in your story?" As the children develop their stories, write them down.
5. When they have finished dictating, read the story back to them. Ask them if they'd like to make any changes to the story. Then ask if they'd like to illustrate the story.

Respond to Individual Needs

1. Make the most of your talented bilingual staff and volunteers by helping children who are dual language learners learn to use some of the ideas in this article. A child can create wonderful stories in his or her home language with a box of familiar items and the help of a bilingual adult who knows how to support early literacy in the child's home language.

2. Some children might need more individualized attention during this activity than others. Prompt them with questions, suggestions, or offer to work with them to write their first story. Once they have created their first couple of stories, they'll feel more comfortable doing this activity.

Follow Up After the Activity

1. Invite children to share their completed stories with the rest of the class. Children could also choose to act out various parts of the story. They may want to use the original shoebox objects as props.

2. Provide several extra shoeboxes so children can fill them with random items and create more stories.

Involve Families

1. Invite families to bring in items from home that can be included in the shoeboxes.

2. Send copies of the stories home with children so that families can read the stories at home with their children.

A Trip to the Book Hospital

Natalie Klein-Raymond

Why do this activity? Have the books in your classroom library seen some wear and tear? Repair class books and learn with preschoolers by setting up a book hospital in a corner of the literacy center.

What can children learn? Children will learn to value and take care of books. Preschoolers will also be looking at letters and words as they repair the books and typically become more excited to revisit books that they have fixed. They will also be building fine motor skills as they make the repairs.

Vocabulary words: *spine, dust jacket, hardcover, paperback, pages, endpapers, binding, hospital*

Materials:

- Nontoxic disinfectant, sponges, and paper towels
- Erasers
- Invisible tape
- Scotch tape
- Heavy-duty book tape (available online from library supply vendors)
- Books that need to be repaired
- Boxes, baskets, and bags to keep the book hospital organized

Prepare for the Activity

1. Fill a container with the tape, erasers, and cleaning materials. This will serve as your book repair kit.
2. Place books that need to be repaired in a box or basket for children to easily find and repair. When selecting books to place in the hospital, look for tears, stray crayon and pencil marks, and worn binding.
3. Clear a space for the children to work. This could be a table or a small space on the carpet. Children should have enough space to move around freely and should be able to hear each other when speaking.

Lead Small Groups

1. Review the book hospital materials and procedures. First, introduce the books that need repair. This may be a good time to explain that the books have been read so many times that they are starting to fall apart, "It's our job to take care of our library and make sure that we fix the books." Then introduce the supplies that children will use to repair the books. Take each

item out of the book repair kit one-by-one and show preschoolers how and when to use them.

2. Have a few children at a time watch you do repairs. First clean dirty books using the cleaning materials. Then erase crayon and pencil marks. Next use invisible tape to repair torn pages, dust jackets, or pop-up flaps and tabs. To repair a broken book spine, open the book in the middle and lay it face down. Apply self-adhesive heavy-duty book tape down the outside of the spine. Apply the book tape to the inside front and back seams.

3. Have children take turns making simple repairs as you look on. Help children as they figure out what each book needs and begin repairs.

Respond to Individual Needs

1. Some preschoolers are still developing the fine motor skills necessary to do this activity. Help them to use the book hospital by scaffolding how they use erasers, scissors, tape, and other materials.

2. Use the activity as an opportunity to help all of the children build their vocabulary.

Follow Up After the Activity

Place repaired books in the literacy center for children to look at. Continue to place books that need repair in the book hospital for children to fix.

Involve Families

1. Ask families to bring in books to be repaired.

2. Suggest that families repair books with their children. Send home instructions and a list of materials needed.

Real-Life Reasons to Write

Louis Mark Romei

I am sure many of us remember sitting at a desk and writing the same alphabet letter over and over again. You may have traced a dotted line several times before writing on your own. But why were we writing that letter? What did it mean? More important, if we had asked our teachers these questions, what would they have said?

As a young preschool teacher, those memories are fresh in my mind. I make sure every classroom writing experience is meaningful for children and has an authentic purpose. Such opportunities help children become skilled and enthusiastic writers.

Each child has his or her own unique method when beginning to write. To respect the styles and skill levels of all of the children, I provide a range of writing activities. Here are some ways preschoolers can have real-life opportunities to write.

Taking attendance

1 Children sign in when arriving at school, just as they see grown-ups do. They use a pencil tied to a string next to the sign-in sheet, posted within their reach.

Making lists

2 When we make a plan for a class party or activity, the children write or dictate a list of what we need. As we receive the items, the children check them off the list.

Writing notes and cards

3 Children regularly make greeting cards for birthdays, holidays, and other occasions, for families, friends, classmates, and teachers. They write thank-you notes to guest speakers and to family members who read to the class, participate on field trips, or take part in other classroom activities. I introduce thank-you notes at the beginning of the year, and soon children are writing them on their own.

Expressing feelings in letters

4 When children have a disagreement, I encourage them each to write a letter to the other person, explaining their thoughts and feelings. Sometimes, if a child is having a bad day, I read *Alexander and the Terrible, Horrible, No Good, Very Bad Day*, by Judith Viorst. Then I suggest that the child draw a picture and sign it, like Alexander does in the story.

Helping to write notes home

5 When writing to ask a child's family for a change of clothes or to tell them about the amazing block structure their child made, I invite the child to help me. I might write a question like, "Can you please send in . . . ?" and then use a think-aloud strategy, for example, pointing out that "I need to use a question mark here because I asked a question." In this way the child sees how punctuation helps make my message clear.

Writing in journals

6 Children write and draw about their favorite parts of the day. They may record things they want to remember or jot down words from the word wall. We post photos with captions that include words pertaining to our current studies. The children refer to the captions when trying to remember the name of a particular object or living creature. This helps children build their vocabularies. Eventually they remember the new words on their own and no longer need to use the photos.

Developing fine motor skills

7 A variety of materials and activity choices let children practice their small muscle skills.

For example, children make three-dimensional letters and words using playdough. They squirt glue in the shape of a letter and shake sand or glitter on top to create letter cards. Later, they can trace the shape of the letter with their fingers. At group time I invite the children to use their bodies to form letters.

Signing up on waiting lists

8 Children are always eager to enter certain learning centers, and they tend to get upset when the area is full. A waiting list works well as a visual prompt for taking turns. It also removes me from the negotiations! Children write their name next to a number on the list. When a classmate leaves the area, she lets the next child know it's his turn. Before entering the area, he places a check mark next to his name, indicating that he is taking his turn in the area.

Contributing to a monthly newsletter

9 Every month each child chooses a topic to write about, and all of the contributions are included in the newsletter. Some children write about the topics we are studying, others describe recent activities, birthday celebrations, or the weather. In some cases, children ask to take a digital photo of a block building or art project to include with a written caption. They help to print the photos using the computer. We work on the newspaper over several weeks before sending it home as a "month in review," such as "October in Review." The more involved the children are in each step of the process, the more excited and motivated they are to write and learn.

Learning from children's literature

10 I read several books by the same author to highlight how writers develop their themes and styles over time. We also discuss how authors repeat favorites or try out new ones. Sometimes we write alternate versions of stories we read during group times. We also make story maps on large pieces of paper to clearly separate the story into the beginning, the middle, and the end. This helps the children see the sequence of events unfold on one sheet of paper. To the story map they can add their own artwork, dictation, and shared writing with the teacher, using vocabulary words and characters from the story.

Supporting Dual Language Learners

The terms *meaningful* and *with authentic purpose* are key to successfully supporting dual language learners. Boring, repetitive, artificial tasks are not worth much, no matter the language. On the other hand, authentic activities that really connect to a child's prior knowledge and home experiences make activities much more effective for all learners. It is worth the extra effort to provide writing models and activities in the home languages of the children. Be sure to focus on real-life examples and things children really want to write about! Research tells us that early literacy skills learned in the home language are likely to transfer easily to English later on, so home language writing activities support success in later grades.

Writing Poetry With Preschoolers

Pamela Hobart Carter

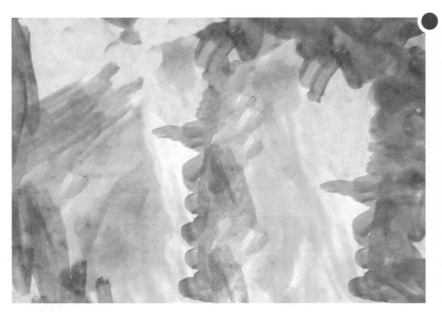

"Pond," by Rosemary

A place in imagination,
hidden from the rest of the world,
peaceful.

I like how its waves roll.
Birds flying, birds cheeping,
grasses waving in the wind.

Play around the edges
when it's sunset,
Ready for anything under the sky.

For the last two years I have been a classroom teacher for the 4- and 5-year-olds group and a poetry specialist for the entire school. When I listen to a child create a poem, I learn which ideas are important to her. I get to hear the surprises she thinks of, many of which would be hidden without my invitation to write a poem. Through this activity, each child learns that inside us all is a poem waiting to be expressed.

Writing Poetry Individualizes the Curriculum

Creating poetry with preschoolers allows them to focus on a specific task. Each child receives my full attention as he expresses his ideas and feelings. We talk back and forth as we discuss, write, and edit the poem. As I write his poem, the child observes how rhythmic oral language can be represented as words on a page—a new purpose for writing. The one-on-one attention allows me to help each child express his ideas and feelings in a way tailored to that individual.

During this process, preschoolers develop a sense of what it means to put words and lines together to make a poem. The individual poems are included in a class book or display. Assisting individual children in writing poetry strengthens their vocabulary, trains their senses, exercises their memory, and tunes their ear. Writing poetry gives me information about a child's vocabulary, ease of speech, sense of rhythm, and understanding of the concept and the assignment.

Individual writing benefits the group. Poetry unites communities and helps us know each other better. Friends and families can read the poems and see expressions of each child's character. It lets all of the preschoolers take pride in their creativity.

Using a Template

My first attempt at helping children write poetry relied on a template borrowed from poet Rachel Zucker. She described creating poetry with children during a visit to her own child's class in a beautiful article, "Third Eye Ode to Chicken Nugget and Other Delights" in

Poetry. Zucker's article gave me a clear method and the help I needed to get started. Now I invent my own templates, and my confidence grows with each poetry experience.

Our school decided to create a poetry book connected to a theme, based on *Oh, the Places You'll Go!*, by Dr. Seuss. The art teacher and I joined forces. With her, the children would draw pictures; with me, they would write poems. Each child would create a page, and together the whole school would create the book.

I developed a loose template for creating poems and tested it with a few children in the class. The inaugural product was Rosemary's poem, which opens this piece. Then I analyzed the steps I took with Rosemary and documented the process. For example, while working with Rosemary, I remembered saying, "Poets often realize that where their thoughts start is not necessarily where the poem starts." This led me to add a step to the poetry process template: "Ask the child which is the start line." Rosemary and I had hopped around in her list of lines so much that I numbered the lines. This led to another step in the process: "Arrange the lines with the child."

"In The Woods," by Ian

I'm in the woods
I'm blending in
If I were in the woods
I'd totally blend in
If something was chasing me
I could just run in my shoes
They're super-fast runners
Maybe like a fox
Brown and white in the back
And white on the tail
It feels good because I
Could just blend into a tree
I would find a brown tree
And stand very still
Ready for anything under the sky!

My Poetry Process Template

1. Read *Oh, the Places You'll Go!* (or a book you like) to the children. Discuss its metaphoric (fill-in-the blank) nature.
2. Introduce the project and give children time to think about it.
3. Ask each child later or on another day to draw something that relates to the book. Our art teacher asked children to draw a picture of a place where they wanted to go.
4. Talk individually with each child about the illustration. Try open-ended questions or comments such as "Tell me about this." For children who are less forthcoming, try an either–or question, such as "Was it warm or cold?"
5. Record the child's comments on paper.
6. Read the lines back to the child.
7. Ask the child which is the start line. Number and arrange the lines with the child. If the poem is very short, repeat steps four through six.
8. Open at random the book used as inspiration and have the child choose a line from it. Check that he likes that line and feels it suits his poem. Decide together where to insert it in the poem. Underline that line (as in the poems in this article).
9. Edit. Suggest cutting words, dropping lines, or repeating certain lines or words. Read the draft aloud. Ask, "Is there anything you want to add or take away?" Edit again.
10. Type the poem or print it neatly. Display or publish it by itself or as part of a collection.

Why I Write Poetry With Preschoolers

I am a poet. Writing poems with children lets me celebrate and share my passion at school. Until I start, I never know how much of a thrill each child-made poem will bring. A thrill because a child who is often quiet produces some words. A thrill because of children's candor and unique phrasing. The process always surprises me, and the children inspire my own poetry. I wish the same for you.

REFERENCE

Zucker, R. 2011. "Third Eye Ode to a Chicken Nugget and Other Delights." *Poetry.* www.poetryfoundation.org/article/241876.

RESOURCE

Poetry Foundation, www.poetryfoundation.org.

"A Secret Garden," by Frances

It's opener there in the wide open air where the grass never grows but where the flowers always bloom every year and the sun shines every day and it's not the Earth, it's on a brand new planet somebody just built. I built it! I have a watch guard for it where I can rest so I can go to sleep so I won't get tired by watching the garden all night.

Reflective Questions

Know Yourself
The author writes, "I am a poet. Writing poems with children lets me celebrate and share my passion at school." What do you think about teachers sharing their personal passions and interests with children? How might this contribute to the teaching and learning process?

Find the Details of Children's Competence
How does the author use the experience of writing poetry to observe and delight in children's competence? How does she use the experience to strengthen relationships with children?

Seek the Children's Point of View
Study the examples of children's poetry given in the article. What draws your curiosity and attention in each of these poems? What feelings or interests might the child author of a poem be exploring?

Conversations With Preschoolers: Learning to Give and Take

Ann S. Epstein

During the preschool years, children are building their conversational skills. They will use these skills to exchange ideas, observations, thoughts, and feelings with family members, peers, and teachers. Having a conversation is a give-and-take activity—sometimes it is your turn to talk and other times you are the listener. It takes lots of practice to develop conversation skills. Much of this practice takes place when teachers have conversations with children.

Here are some strategies for engaging preschoolers in meaningful two-way conversations.

- **Model active listening as well as talking.** Preschoolers are not always fluent in their speech. Wait patiently while they frame and express their thoughts. Get down on their level and make eye contact. Listen carefully, then repeat or clarify what they say. To keep the conversation going, summarize their thoughts and then expand on their ideas.
- **Help children build listening skills.** Play games that use verbal directions, such as Simon Says. The gestures that go with the verbal directions are especially helpful for dual language learners. They help them understand body and action vocabulary words.

- **Speak clearly.** Model standard language (vocabulary and pronunciation, grammar and syntax). Use more complex sentences as children's verbal skills increase.
- **Expand on children's comments.** For example, if a preschooler says, "More juice," you might say, "You'd like Katelyn to pass you the pitcher." Expanding a one- or two-word statement into a short sentence is especially valuable for dual language learners. It builds on their language in context and is, thus, easier to understand.
- **Hold conversations throughout the day.** Meal and snack times are good opportunities for conversations. During activities and choice time, talk with children about what they have done and what they plan to do next. Start and end the day with conversations. Talk with children about their interests, plans, and experiences.
- **Encourage children to talk to one another.** Plan group activities that promote playing and working together rather than alone. To support peer conversations redirect children's attention to one

another. Next, restate the topic of the conversation and suggest they share ideas. Provide props for role playing and pretending. The desire to join in such play motivates dual language learners to communicate in a way that their peers can understand. Often they will observe and listen intently, and then try out their emerging English-speaking skills so they can join in.

- **Ask questions, but not too many.** Use them to invite children to think and give detailed responses. Avoid questions that have a single or brief correct answer.

Questions and Comments That Open—or Close Down—Children's Thinking

Sometimes adults ask children questions to which they already know the answer. For example, if a teacher asks, "What color is your sweater?" she is likely to know that it is blue or red. The question is more of a test than an invitation to talk. To encourage children to think and expand their answers and learn new words, ask open-ended questions that could be answered in different ways by different children. Such questions truly communicate that you want to hear children's ideas or learn about their experiences. Some examples appear below.

Questions or comments that encourage children to think and reason, and use expanded language:

- "How can you tell?"
- "How do you know that?"
- "What do you think made that happen?"
- "How did you make that?"
- "I wonder would happen if . . . ?"
- "How can you get it to stick [or roll or stand up]?"

Examples of questions that introduce vocabulary words and concepts:

- "How can we move the truck [or ball or sand] *without* using our hands?" (If children respond only with motions, label the body parts and movements children suggest.)
- "Kenisha says we can put the bowl [or wet painting or seed cup] on top of the shelf or inside her cubby. Where else do you think we can store it so people don't bump into it?"
- "Antoine says he sees a lot of monkeys in this picture. I count five of them. (Point to and count each one.) What else do you see a lot of?"
- "What kinds of fruits do people in your family like to eat?"
- "What things in the science area [or house area or block area] are heavy? Which do you think is the *heaviest*? How could we find out?"

Get to Know the
New Children's Librarian

Karen N. Nemeth and Cen Campbell

When is the last time you talked to a children's librarian? If it's been a while, this is a great time to strike up a conversation. You might be surprised at the innovative activities, programs, and services children's librarians offer preschool teachers, young children, and families. With new and diverse materials and resources, librarians make wonderful partners for educators as they plan ways to meet each child's individual needs. Librarians provide three main services: collections, outreach, and programs.

Collections

A big collection of books is still a library's most important feature, but libraries also function as new media leaders. Libraries offer music collections, audio books, and computer games. Many even lend tablets or eReaders preloaded with librarian-curated content. Libraries also take recommendations from the community. Teachers who need books or other materials for their program can ask their local library to purchase them.

- Preschool teachers in New Brunswick, New Jersey, visit their local library often to borrow children's books, travel books, music, cookbooks, and other resources in Hungarian, Spanish, Portuguese, Chinese, and many other languages needed in their diverse classrooms. When families who speak a new language enroll in their program, the teachers ask the librarians for more resources in that language.

Outreach

Bringing library services to community organizations that serve children is a core principle of children's librarianship. Librarians are eager to reach out and meet the changing needs of their community. They want to know the families in their area and find new ways to bring them to the library.

Many library systems have bookmobiles or delivery vans that provide books, bilingual resources, multimedia resources, and even Internet access. Some bookmobiles or other mobile library services stop at preschools and offer story time or other literacy programs.

- Nicki Carteaux, director of a Head Start program in Ligonier, Indiana, learned that her local library was offering literacy services at local preschools. She arranged for the children's librarian to visit the Head Start center weekly to present an early literacy program, engage teachers and children in a related activity, and deliver a borrowed-book bag for children to take home.

- The Pierce County Library System in Tacoma, Washington, lists resources for teachers on their website, including professional development classes, an oral health project, and a block project. The library also runs Ready for Books, a program that delivers books and resource materials to local preschool programs.
- In remote Bridgetown, Nova Scotia (population 1,000), in Canada, the Annapolis Valley regional library provides mobile library services to schools and preschools. Each of the 11 branches in Annapolis Valley has an individualized relationship with preschools in their service areas. Angela Reynolds, head of children's services for the regional library, also helps connect libraries and schools by teaching early childhood education classes at the local community college.

Programs

- Children's librarians are experts at choosing high-quality books and media for young children. They have been using developmentally appropriate practice in story times and literacy programming for a long time.
- NAEYC's Week of the Young Child, which takes place every April, coincides with El día de los niños/El día de los libros (Children's Day/Book Day), often called Día. Founded by author Pat Mora, Día celebrates diversity through children, families, and reading every day. It culminates yearly on April 30 and is often celebrated all month long.
- Every Child Ready to Read is a literacy-based parent education initiative sponsored by the American Library Association. It helps families and teachers support early literacy development at home and at school with books and ebooks.

New Media for Young Children

Children's librarians are leaders in using new media with young children. They are up-to-date with recent ebooks and apps and how to incorporate those tools into traditional early literacy programming. Librarians are trained experts in evaluating and curating reading materials. They can help others find and use the best apps, websites, and software for individuals and for groups of preschoolers. In turn, websites and communities such as LittleeLit.com support children's librarians as they advance into the digital realm.

Library websites may also offer additional electronic resources. Many libraries subscribe to programs that feature digital books and extension activities, such as TumbleBookLibrary (www.tumblebooks.com/) and BookFlix (http://teacher.scholastic.com/products/bookflix freetrial/index.htm). These programs also feature books in different languages so each child can learn in a way that fits his needs.

- The library in Darien, Connecticut, offers early literacy iPad kits that can be checked out and taken home, as well as digital storytelling programs and an array of resources for teachers about using new media with young children.

Funding Solutions

When applying for a grant or special funding, teachers may gain from partnering with another organization—including the local library. Not only does this show funders a willingness to work within the community, but it can also maximize or extend a limited budget.

- Alpine County Library in Markleeville, California, addressed a tight budget by partnering with a local nonprofit organization that provides innovative child care solutions in communities where many families have low incomes. The organization sends staff to the library to implement early literacy programming, while the Friends of the Library group supplies materials.

Conclusion

Librarians strengthen and connect their communities by providing up-to-date information, resources, and programming to teachers working with young children. Children's librarians always want to hear about what children and teachers are working on and how they can help. When you partner with a children's librarian, you will find new ways to individualize early literacy and learning for each child in your program.

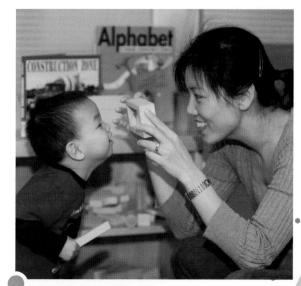

Using Multiple Texts to Guide Children's Learning

Meagan K. Shedd

A child asks, "What do I do with this yogurt cup?" Later that day, children huddle over a book about recycling. They discuss plans for constructing a recycling center in the dramatic play area. When several children wonder how to create a conveyor belt, one young builder decides to consult a book. After finding a page with the needed information, his teacher reads aloud a text box and a photo caption. Another child offers a pamphlet from the local recycling facility. The pamphlet has photos of a conveyor belt. Together, the children review the photos to see what new information the brochure provides.

For nearly 14 weeks, this question, "How can we create a conveyor belt?" inspires and guides activities in a project-based classroom as the children create a recycling center.

The children study recycling, reusing, and reducing waste. Their study evolves in response to a question about whether an everyday yogurt container goes in the trash can or the recycling bin.

esearchers say it is important to have multiple types of texts in early childhood education settings (Duke 2007). Children need to understand and write many different kinds of text. These include storybooks and nonfiction books, along with letters, newspapers, magazines, recipes and other kinds of instructions, and print from developmentally appropriate websites and apps.

Ms. Pattengill and Mrs. Elm, the teachers in this classroom, thoughtfully consider what kinds of texts to share with the children and what techniques to use when reading aloud. When reading a poem, for example, they emphasize the lyrical rhythms by reading with expression. They pause at the end of lines to emphasize when two words rhyme.

Finding Information

When helping children look for information in a nonfiction book, the teachers model how to flip through the pages, looking for photos and captions, text boxes, and diagrams. This lets the children learn about, use, and enjoy each type of text. During the recycling project, the children looked up facts in informational texts, such as *Recycle That!*, by Fay Robinson. Listening to poetry about recycling showed them that poems can be both informative and fun.

Supporting Text Use

We read and use different types of texts in many ways. Some we read cover to cover; others are sources for specific information. Teachers can move about the

classroom, noting how children use different kinds of texts. If necessary, a teacher might model how to use a book. For example, Mrs. Elm explained, "We need an informational book to answer that question. The title of this book is *Recycle That!* Let's look at the table of contents to see if there is a chapter on conveyor belts. I don't see one, so now let's look in the index. Yes, here it is." She then showed the children a photo with a caption that was just as important as the text on the page. It had the information the children needed to build the conveyor belt.

To introduce an art activity using recycled objects, Ms. Pattengill read the book's introduction to help the children think about what materials they could use for their creations. Ms. Pattengill said, "Look at the pictures in the book. Can you think of ways to use the objects in front of you?" This helped the children connect the text to the activity. As small groups of children worked on their projects, they came up with other ways to use the items. Ms. Pattengill offered encouraging comments like, "The book says you can do that too" and "You came up with an idea they didn't have here!"

Reading Nonfiction

Teachers do not have to read nonfiction texts like they do stories, which are read from front to back. Recipes, magazines, newspapers, and websites can provide similar, nonlinear reading experiences. These texts may be less familiar to some children, so teachers use their fingers to point to words or show how to use specific parts of the text. Just as a teacher would model how text or print concepts work in a storybook, it is important to do the same with nonfiction texts. For example, a teacher would explain that the table of contents tells us what is in the book and on which page to find the information.

Stocking the Learning Centers

To help children understand the purpose of different types of texts, a typical preschool classroom should include 1/3 narrative, 1/3 informational, and 1/3 other kinds of texts (Duke 2007). Place books in the literacy center and in other learning centers. You can take a basket with a variety of books outdoors.

Include the following in the literacy center:

- Five to eight books per child. Offer books with diverse characters and topics, and books that match the literacy levels of the children in the classroom (Bennett-Armistead, Duke, & Moses 2005).
- Books with vibrant illustrations or photographs in addition to appropriate text
- Other reading materials, such as magazines, newspapers, recorded books, and flannel boards that include characters and text from stories or books. Also provide comfortable seating, storage for the various types of texts, and audioplayers and headphones (Bennett-Armistead, Duke, & Moses 2005).

Here are some ideas for including books and other texts in learning centers:

- **Blocks:** Include informational books about buildings or construction such as *Good Night, Good Night Construction Site*, by Sherri Dusker Rinker, *A Year at a Construction Site*, by Nicholas Harris, and Tana Hoban's *Construction Zone*. Blueprints and job lists from construction sites are also relevant.

- **Math and manipulatives:** Look for books with counting concepts, such as Anthony Browne's *One Gorilla* and *Ten Black Dots*, by Donald Crews. Books with photographs, such as *Shapes*, by Ann Peat, illustrate concepts about shapes and size. Leo Lionni's *Inch by Inch* lets children learn about distance and measurement.

- **Dramatic play:** Provide texts that match the themes the children are exploring. For a veterinarian's office, add storybooks like *Mog and the V.E.T.*, by Judith Kerr, or informational books such as *ER Vets: Life in an Animal Emergency Room*, by Donna Jackson. Add a poetry book such the *National Geographic Book of Animal Poetry*. Include children's magazines in the waiting room and offer materials children can use to make signs and charts for "patients."

- **Discovering science:** Add information books, storybooks, and other types of texts about new concepts. During the study of recycling, children enjoyed the storybook *Michael Recycle*, by Ellie Bethel, and the informational text *Composting: Nature's Recyclers*, by Robin Koontz. Anna Alter's *What Can You Do With an Old Red Shoe* is another option.

- **Writing center:** Include each type of text and favorite storybooks read aloud at group time, along with mail, brochures, and phone books to provide informational text. As children learn about poetry, add books like *Here's a Little Poem*, by Jane Yolen.

Different Types of Texts

- **Narrative books** have characters, settings (place and time), problems, events, and solutions. This category includes wordless picture books that meet the criteria using illustrations or photographs, traditional narratives or storybooks, mysteries, pattern books, folktales, and fairy tales.

- **Informational texts** have a primary purpose. They convey information about the natural and social worlds. Typically, the authors know a lot about the subject. This category includes dictionaries, concept books, and wordless picture books that use lifelike illustrations or photographs to provide information.

- **Other types of texts** include items that do not meet the definition of informational or narrative texts. This category includes poetry books, songbooks, nursery rhyme books, graphic novels, biographies, autobiographies, and interactive books such as the I Spy series or *Press Here*, by Herve Tullet.

Conclusion

During the recycling project, Mrs. Elm and Ms. Pattengill continued to add new and different texts to the classroom. When the children completed the recycling center, it included not only a conveyor belt, but also several sorting boxes, a fork truck to "drive" the sorting boxes from one end of the center to the other, and bright orange vests (like those worn by recycling center employees) made by the children from construction paper. Three types of texts had allowed the children to address their inquiry in a meaningful way.

REFERENCES

Bennett-Armistead, V.S., N.K. Duke, & A.M. Moses. 2005. *Literacy and the Youngest Learner: Best Practices for Educators of Children From Birth to 5*. New York: Scholastic.

Duke, N.K. 2007. "Let's Look in a Book: Using Nonfiction Texts for Reference With Young Children." *Young Children* 62 (3): 12–16.

Supporting Dual Language Learners

It's important to represent the home languages of children in the various types of print available in the classroom. If some languages are more difficult to find, ask parents or volunteers to translate at least the key words in fiction and nonfiction books, displays, and other kinds of texts. Type the translated words onto sticker labels to add to your English-only items. Color code the languages so you and the children will always know that a certain color represents a certain language.

Resources for Identifying Wonderful Books

T here are more than 250,000 children's books in print, and each year US publishers add close to 30,000 new books to this total. In addition, individual and library collections include high-quality books that are out of print but still terrific. It is no wonder that many preschool teachers could use some help to identify which of the many great books are a good fit for the preschoolers they teach. The following resources offer reviews and recommendations of classics, award winners, and future favorite titles.

Blogs

Children's Book-a-Day Almanac, by Anita Silvey—http://childrensbookalmanac.com

A book recommendation every day! This site also provides excerpts, reviews, and notes about historic events related to the day.

Seven Impossible Things Before Breakfast, by Julie "Jules" Danielson—http://blaine.org/sevenimpossiblethings

Named for the Lewis Carroll quote, this blog offers frequent picture book reviews.

Public Libraries

Library of Congress site for children's books—http://read.gov/kids

It's especially helpful to ask your local librarian for suggestions related to particular topics.

Lists

Indie Bound—www.indiebound.org/kids-indie-next-list

A top-10 list of the best children's books, recommended by owners of independent bookstores.

New York Times—http://topics.nytimes.com/topics/reference/timestopics/subjects/c/childrens_books/index.html

Reviews from the New York Times Book Review.

Cooperative Children's Book Center—http://ccbc.education.wisc.edu/books/bibBio.asp

Books grouped under topics such as family, sports, and change.

Bank Street College of Education Children's Book Committee—http://bankstreet.edu/cbc

Has a monthly featured children's book, a children's book of the year, and a young reviewers section with honest reviews of books by children who have read them.

Association/Organization Websites

Children's Book Council—www.cbcbooks.org/reading-lists

A book list focusing mainly on science, social studies, and general literacy.

The Global Fund for Children—www.globalfundforchildren.org/store/books-for-children/

More than 250 picture book recommendations, organized by category or theme, highlighting diversity, tolerance, and global citizenship.

Author Websites

If you like one book by an author, consult the author's website to find his or her other books.

Eric Carle—www.eric-carle.com

A list of books, lessons, and resources inspired by Eric Carle's books

Rosemary Wells—www.rosemarywells.com

Events, books, and online games from the author of Max and Ruby books.

Monica Brown—www.monicabrown.net

Books, resources for teachers, and information in Spanish from author Monica Brown.

Authors and Illustrators on the Web—http://people.ucalary.ca/~dkbrown/authors.html

Part of the Children's Literature Web Guide, this page offers an alphabetic list of children's authors' and illustrators' websites

Kirkus Reviews

www.kirkusreviews.com/book-reviews/childrens-books

"The world's toughest book critics" give a great critics' recommendation list!

International Children's Digital Library

http://en.childrenslibrary.org/

This collection offers over 4,000 children's books in 55 languages available to read online. For advice on choosing books in different languages for your classroom, visit www.colorincolorado.org or www.languagelizard.com.

Annual Award Winners

Caldecott Medal—www.ala.org/ala/mgrps/divs/alsc/awardsgrants/bookmedia/caldecottmedal/caldecottmedal.cfm

Awarded to the artist of the best US picture book.

(Theodor Seuss) Geisel Award—www.ala.org/ala/mgrps/divs/alsc/awardsgrants/bookmedia/geiselaward/index.cfm

Given to the author(s) and illustrator(s) of the best US book for beginning readers.

Coretta Scott King Book Award—www.ala.org/ala/mgrps/rts/emiert/cskbookawards/index.cfm

For books by African American authors and illustrators who make outstanding, inspirational, and educational contributions, promoting cultural understanding.

Pura Belpré Award—www.ala.org/ala/mgrps/divs/alsc/awardsgrants/bookmedia/belpremedal/index.cfm

Honoring a Latino/Latina author and illustrator whose work celebrates Latino culture in children's literature.

The Horn Book

www.hbook.com

Publication dedicated entirely to finding good children's books, including author and illustrator profiles as well as book reviews and recommendations.

Young Children and *Teaching Young Children* children's book review columns

"The Reading Chair"—www.naeyc.org/yc/columns/readingchair

A column in every issue of *Young Children* that offers reviews of quality picture books.

"Now Read This!"—*Teaching Young Children (TYC)* column

A themed page of short book reviews and related activities appears in every issue of *TYC*.

Rap and Young Children: Encouraging Preschoolers' Emergent Literacy

Barbara Rando, Evelyn A. O'Connor, Karen Steuerwalt, and Michelle Bloom

Teachers frequently look for ways to motivate and encourage preschoolers' language and literacy learning. One engaging strategy is to create raps with children. By combining music and language, creating and learning raps can help preschoolers understand print concepts and gain phonemic awareness. In addition, the unique rhythm and chanting of raps promotes children's oral language skills.

Creating a Rap

The raps we created with young children focused on historical figures. Here are the steps we took:

1. Choose an important and relevant figure who is of interest to the children.
2. Identify, read aloud, and discuss a biography written for children about the person.
3. Invite the children to recall or find new information about the person. (This information will be the content of the rap.)
4. Compose the rap, write it on chart paper, and display it in the room.

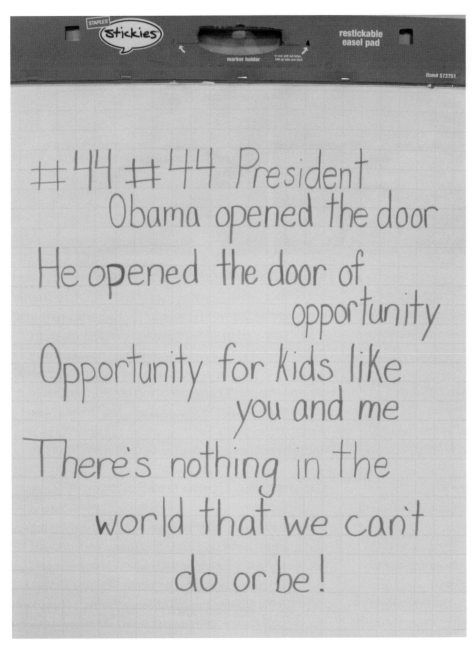

Creating the President Obama Rap

Michelle used the rap-writing process with the preschoolers she taught. Knowing of the children's interest in the president, Barack Obama was chosen as the topic of the rap. Michelle read aloud the biography *Barack Obama: Son of Promise, Child of Hope* (2008), by Nikki Grimes. Because it was a book written for older children, she adapted the book to make it age appropriate for preschoolers. After the read aloud, Michelle guided a discussion using the illustrations and the children's comments about what the illustrations depicted. On chart paper, she recorded what the children said they had learned about President Obama.

Her next task was to combine the children's rec-ollections and make them rhyme. The result was the following Barack Obama rap. Soon the children were eagerly chanting the rap.

#44 #44, President Obama opened the door.
He opened the door of opportunity.
Opportunity for kids like you and me.
There's nothing in the world that we can't do or be!

Introducing New Vocabulary

When Michelle discussed the President Obama rap with the children, she asked them what *opportunity* meant. No one knew. It was not an easy meaning to convey. Michelle found times throughout the day to highlight the use of *opportunity* (for example, men-tioning to the children that they have the opportunity to eat lunch on schedule or to delay it in order to finish

a story). Over time, the children began to make sense of the concept. They learned they could substitute *chance* or *choice* for the word *opportunity*. Michelle knew that 4-year-old Jordan understood the concept when, in the middle of reading a story, Michelle noticed that it was time to pack up to go home. When she told the children that they had to stop and get ready to leave, Jordan called out, "Oh, no we don't, Mrs. Bloom. We don't have to stop now. We have an opportunity to stop and get ready quicker or choose to finish!"

Connecting Home and School

Just as preschoolers can easily learn the words to songs they like, children can remember the rhythms and rhymes of the raps and share them with oth-ers. Jenny, a 4-year-old in Michelle's class, had been quiet since the school year began in September. After learning the Obama rap in February, Jenny initiated a conversation with Michelle: "I told my mommy I was singing the Barack Obama song!" Before this, Jenny had never started a conversation with her teacher. When Barbara visited the classroom, Jenny engaged her in conversation as well. The rap was so exciting and fun for Jenny that, in addition to rapping the piece, she wanted to talk about it. These self-initiated conversations became a way for Michelle to evaluate Jenny's learning. It was evident that rapping was an effective strategy for Jenny because it gave her something to talk about and made her feel comfortable enough to engage in conversation. This momentous experience could be used as a bridge between home and school when planning ways to support Jenny's learning in the future.

Conclusion

Composing and reciting raps can introduce many important literacy skills. When creating the raps, children retold details from the story. They learned the conventions of conversations: to listen and take turns. Chanting the raps contributed to their understanding of phrasing, fluency, intonation, and rhythm in speech.

Every child in the class found success on one level or another. Since the children repeated the raps daily, all the children could recite them from memory and took pride in their accomplishments. The project's effects went beyond the classroom. Families told Michelle that the children came home and rapped to them. Parents asked if the children were performing the rap in an assembly and commented on how excited their children were about the rap and what they learned about President Obama.

Magazines for Preschoolers

As they do with books, teachers can read magazine articles to the class as a whole or to small groups or leave the issues out for children to explore on their own. Some magazines focus on literacy, others on nature, and some include both. As children get to know a particular magazine, they look forward to reading their favorite features in each issue.

Highlights High Five. **Highlights for Children. 12 issues a year. Ages 2–6.**

Stories, poems, comic strips, and activities appear in each issue. Highlights also offers High Five Bilingüe for children learning to speak and read in both English and Spanish. (Discounted subscriptions are available to new and renewing NAEYC members.)

Ladybug. **Cricket Magazine Group. 9 issues a year. Ages 3–6.**

This publication offers illustrated stories; recurring characters and poems, songs, and how-to activity ideas to engage young learners. Each issue includes a removable activity section.

National Geographic Little Kids. **National Geographic Society. 6 issues a year. Ages 3–6.**

Sized for small hands, this magazine is packed with color photographs, animal stories, features about different cultures, simple science activities, and puzzles and games. Each issue includes questions and activities preschoolers can do at home or in the classroom.

Ranger Rick Jr. **National Wildlife Federation. 10 issues a year. Ages 4–7.**

Through color photos and stories children learn about nature, animals, and the world around them. Included are games and fun activities for young children.

Ideas for Teachers

All these magazines provide activities for children. Here are some ideas teachers can try.

Focus on magazine formats. Children can become familiar with each publication's predictable format. Introduce the different parts of a magazine, like the table of contents, articles and recurring columns, and callouts (the large text in circles or boxes).

Talk about favorite features. After children have had a chance to read a few issues, ask them about their favorite sections of the magazine. Some may like the comics, others the stories or poems, and still others the games and activity ideas. Learning what you like to read is part of becoming an engaged reader.

Build a classroom lending library. Create a magazine library so families can take home back issues, read them together, and try out some of the activities. Families who receive their own subscriptions might want to contribute their back issues to the library as well.

Find out more. Did the children see an animal that they want to learn more about? A fact that intrigues them? Look for more information in books or websites. List the facts the children learn on a large whiteboard. Revisit the magazine story that inspired their research and compare it to the new facts the children discovered.

Supporting Dual Language Learners

Children's magazines add a fun, new dimension to early reading and researching activities. Some are available or have material in Spanish. When you are not able to find appropriate magazines in the languages used by the class, try modifying English versions. Translate key words onto small labels and stick them on the pages. If you can't find an exact translation, look online to find another children's poem, song, or story on a similar topic written in the needed language. Or get everyone involved by creating a class magazine with translations from families, other staff, and volunteers.

Nontraditional Books to Engage Emergent Readers

Linda Dauksas and Kathleen Chvostal-Schmidt

One effective way to promote preschoolers' literacy skills is for teachers, children, and families to make and read their own books. Creating stories with real objects and toys offers a playful and appropriate transition to printed materials. The 10 types of nontraditional books described here will engage young children. They will also help them discover how using pictures, photographs, writing, and reading lets everyone share experiences and retell favorite stories. Children can make and read books in the classroom, at home with their families, or during a family event at the program. All the books are easily made with everyday, recyclable materials. Children can create them on their own, with each other, or with help from an adult.

1 Container books
Create a story by gathering small objects or manipulatives in a container such as a box, basket, or carton. Attach some related photos to the outside. Even the youngest storyteller can carry his or her story around the room and outdoors.

2 Chalk talk
Write and illustrate a story outside on the sidewalk. Each sidewalk square can serve as a page. Walk and read the story aloud.

3 Grocery bag big books
Tape large paper grocery bags together with the plain side of the bag on the outside. Use loose-leaf rings to connect as many pages as needed. Draw or glue on pictures, and add words to create a big book. (If you don't have any paper grocery bags, use a roll of brown wrapping paper or large sheets of thick paper.)

4 **Plastic zipper-bag books**

Gather objects, photographs, or pictures cut from magazines or printed from a colorful website. Create the pages by putting each object or picture in a sandwich- or snack-size plastic zipper bag. Depending on the content, you can seal the bags permanently or leave them open. If left open, the "author" can change the pages—and the story—as needed. Bind the bags to make a book using loose-leaf rings or duct tape.

5 **Sequencing story**

Fold a long rectangular piece of paper accordion style. Add pictures or words on each section of the paper to tell a story. This format is especially appropriate for teaching each step of a task (brushing teeth, getting dressed). Read the book by unfolding the paper from left to right or top to bottom.

6 **Block books**

Tape pictures and words to wooden or plastic blocks, then stack them or line them up to reveal a story. Leave the blocks in the block center so children can make stories while playing with the blocks. Change the pictures and words when they get torn or as children's interests change.

7 **Stick story**

Write simple sentences on tongue depressors. They can be lines from a nursery rhyme or part of a story the class makes up. Attach a corresponding object or picture to one end of each stick. Use as many sticks as needed to tell the story. Attach the sticks in order, using a ribbon or piece of yarn.

8 **Story totes**

Place photographs, pictures, and words inside mittens, socks, purses, backpacks, or plastic bottles. Remove the pictures and words, then arrange or sequence them to tell a story.

9 **Placemat stories**

Write and illustrate a story on large pieces of construction paper. Laminate the papers and place them in sequence on the table during meal or snack time. As children walk around the table, they can read the story.

10 **Seasonal tales**

Write a story or glue pictures on a beach ball, inflated ring, birdhouse, plastic pumpkin, bucket, or other seasonal toy. Each object can hold memories and tell the story of a fun-filled day.

Helping Preschoolers Prepare for Writing:
Developing Fine Motor Skills

J. Michelle Huffman and Callie Fortenberry

A preschool teacher, Ms. Baker, holds a conference with Mr. and Mrs. Lucio to discuss their daughter Mari's interests, activities, and progress. Ms. Baker shares stories and work samples that show how Mari is inquisitive, creative, and intelligent and is building strong literacy skills. She can identify all uppercase and lowercase letters, knows the sounds in individual words (phonemic awareness), and recognizes many sight words. However, Mari has great difficulty writing her name.

The parents' frustration and confusion are evident. At home Mari has pencils and paper, and both parents have done all they know to do to help her master this skill. Why is Mari struggling to write her name?

Ms. Baker reassures Ms. Lucio. She explains that Mari is still developing the fine motor skills needed for writing. She is making progress, on her own individual and appropriate schedule for development.

by providing fine motor tasks that help all children succeed. For example, children can pour water from one container to another or squeeze water from a turkey baster, clip clothespins on a plastic cup, string beads, and tear paper.

Throughout the day, you can nurture children's emerging fine motor skills by providing materials and activities that support children during each stage of physical development. With planning and preparation, preschool classrooms can provide opportunities for children to develop the fine motor skills used for writing and a number of other tasks.

Activities That Promote Fine Motor Development

Simple activities that help children gain the skills needed for writing appear on the next two pages.

REFERENCES

Adolph, K.E. 2008. "Motor/Physical Development: Locomotion." In *Encyclopedia of Infant and Early Childhood Development*, 359–73. San Diego, CA: Academic Press.

Carvell, N.R. 2006. *Language Enrichment Activities Program (LEAP)*, vol. 1. Dallas, TX: Southern Methodist University.

C hildren use their fine motor skills when learning to write. Before preschoolers can write, they need to develop the small muscles in their hands and arms so that they can hold and control markers, chunky crayons, and other writing instruments.

Preschoolers follow a typical sequence in developing small muscles. They usually begin with whole-arm movements and progress toward very detailed fine motor control at the fingertips (Adolph 2008). As young children do activities such as painting a refrigerator box with paint rollers and water or tossing a beach ball into a laundry basket, they use their entire arm. These whole-arm movements lead to building the smaller muscles in their hands.

Fine motor skills are difficult for preschoolers to master, because the skills depend on muscular control, patience, judgment, and brain coordination (Carvell 2006). You can support children's muscle development

Muscle Development	Activity and Materials	Description
WHOLE ARM	**Under-the-Table Art** Large sheet of drawing paper, tape, and crayons	Tape the paper to the underside of a table. Children lie on their backs under the table, extend the arm with crayon or chalk in hand, and draw on the paper.
	Ribbons and Rings Set of plastic bracelets and 12 inches of colored ribbon for each bracelet	Tie one ribbon to each bracelet. Play music. Children wear or hold their bracelet, using their bracelet arm to make big circles, wave the ribbons high and low, and perform other creative movements.
	Stir It Up! Large pot, long wooden spoon, and beads or pebbles	Put the "ingredients" and the spoon in the bowl, and place in the dramatic play area. Children "stir the soup" using a large circular arm motion.
WHOLE HAND	**Sponge Squeeze** Small sponge, divided food dish, and water	Fill one side of the dish with water. Children move the water from side to the other by dipping and squeezing the sponge.
	Lid Match Two baskets and a collection of plastic containers with matching lids (spice jars, margarine tubs, yogurt cups, shampoo containers, hand cream jars, and such)	Sort the containers and lids into separate baskets. Children match and attach the lids to the right containers.
	Sand Sifting Crank-style sifter, 1-cup plastic measuring cup, large bowl, and sand	Place the empty sifter in the bowl. Children use two hands to pour the sand into the sifter, then turn the crank handle to sift the sand into the bowl.

Muscle Development	Activity and Materials	Description
PINCHER	**Button Drop** Four plastic containers with lids, and buttons	Cut a slit in each lid and label each container with a color. Children sort the buttons by color and drop them into the appropriate containers.
	Color Transfer Eyedroppers, muffin tin, food coloring, water, and a section of rubber bath mat backed with suction cups	Fill the muffin tin compartments with water of different colors. Children use the eyedroppers to drop colored water into each suction cup.
	Using Tongs Spring-handle metal tongs, sorting trays (ice cube trays, egg cartons, divided dishes, small containers), and items to sort (counting bears, acorns, buttons, pom-poms)	Show children how to use their thumb and middle and index fingers to manipulate the tongs. Children use the tongs to pick up the items and sort them into separate compartments or containers.
PINCER	**Capture the Cork!** Corks in a variety of sizes, a bowl of water, and tweezers	Put the corks in the bowl of water. Children use the tweezers to try to capture the floating corks.
	Locks and Keys A variety of small locks with keys	Close the locks. Children try to determine which keys work with which locks and unlock them.
	Clip It A variety of small barrettes, hair clips, and elastic bands; dolls with hair, brushes, combs, and a tray for materials	Children use the hair fasteners or elastic bands to divide the dolls' hair into small sections. Clips that fasten in different ways and small elastic bands support a range of motor skill levels.

Adapted with permission from Nell R. Carvell, *Language Enrichment Activities Program (LEAP)*, vol. 1 (Dallas, TX: Southern Methodist University, 2006).

Talk Now, Read Later

Laura J. Colker

Four-year-old Louisa sits with her teacher at the lunch table. Trying to engage her in conversation, the teacher, Ms. Norman, asks, "What did you think of this morning's field trip to the Itsy, Bitsy Bakery?" "It was nice," responds Louisa. "What did you like about it?" asks Ms. Norman. "I liked those big things they put the flour and stuff in." "Oh yes, those mixers were amazing," she agrees. "Did you see what else they put in the mixers?" "I seen one person put in eggs and milk." "I saw that too, Louisa. I thought it was very interesting to watch her put in those ingredients to make dough."

Recent research on the use of language in preschool classrooms has exciting implications for preschool teachers. Educators have long been aware of the link between children's oral language skills and later reading comprehension. However, what these exact skills are and how they relate to reading have been largely unknown. New research by David Dickinson of Vanderbilt University and Michelle Porche of Wellesley College (Dickinson 2011; Dickinson & Porche 2011) provides useful information about the relationship between oral language and reading skills.

The Research

Researchers audiotaped, videotaped, and observed teachers and preschoolers from communities in which many families have low incomes to determine the types of classroom language experiences children had. They were particularly interested in how teachers introduced vocabulary, the complexity of words spoken by teachers and children, and the situations during which children talked with teachers. Researchers then examined data showing the content and quantity of children's language.

The children in the study were followed through elementary school to see the effects of these early language experiences on children's later literacy skills. Specifically, researchers reassessed the children's language and literacy skills at the end of kindergarten and in fourth grade. What the researchers found was that even with a small sample size (57 children), there was a "robust" relationship between early classroom support for language and later language and reading ability (Wetzel 2011, 2). In other words, those preschool children whose teachers supported their oral language skills through conversations and read-alouds were consistently better speakers and readers in kindergarten and fourth grade.

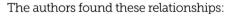

The authors found these relationships:

- Preschool teachers' use of rich and interesting vocabulary is positively linked to kindergartners' ability to successfully use and read books.
- Preschool teachers' use of complex vocabulary words during informal conversations with children leads to improved word recognition and advanced reading comprehension in fourth grade.
- Reading aloud in groups during preschool is linked to high reading comprehension skills in fourth grade.
- Teacher–child conversations that included analysis of stories and discussions of word meanings, along with teachers' gentle corrections of children's non-standard grammar and word forms, are positively correlated with children's increased knowledge of vocabulary in both kindergarten and fourth grade.
- Preschool teachers' abilities to hold children's attention in both read-alouds and conversations are also linked to better reading comprehension in fourth grade.

What This Means for You

This research tells preschool teachers that your frequent and meaningful verbal interactions with children will help them to be good readers in the future. Knowing this, you can continue to use effective teaching practices and add new ones that help children gain strong language and literacy skills.

Consider the anecdote at the beginning of this article. What did Louisa's teacher do to promote her oral language skills? First, she engaged her in a one-on-one conversation in an informal atmosphere. When Louisa gave her a short reply, she tried to coax her into talking further. She gave a name to the objects she described—*mixer*—adding another word to her vocabulary. When

Louisa said *seen* instead of *saw*, she modeled correct grammar by saying, "I saw that too." She did this naturally, without drawing attention to the mistake. She concluded by giving Louisa two new rich vocabulary words—*ingredients* and *dough*—and defined them as being related to what Louisa saw at the bakery. Encounters like these will support Louisa's learning in preschool, and in kindergarten and beyond.

All preschool teachers can use teaching practices that help children build strong oral skills. Here are some strategies that are supported by Dickinson and Porche's research findings:

- Hold one-on-one conversations with children. Talks during learning center time and at lunch have proven to be most effective. "Portia, you mixed a vivid shade of green. It's called chartreuse. What colors did you combine?"
- Read aloud to children several times a day. Pick books that feature interesting vocabulary. During read-alouds, discuss the plot, the characters, the actions, and the feelings evoked by the story and the illustrations. Encourage children to ask and answer questions and share their ideas. "Ryan, what did you think the frog was going to do? Were you surprised?"

- Introduce children to rich, exciting vocabulary and use it in context. This allows children to understand what words mean from the way they are used in the conversation. "The snow is falling so fast it looks like a blizzard."
- Use a low-key and nonjudgmental approach to respond to children's mistakes in grammar and word usage. Model correct usage in your responses. "Tell us more about when you *went* to the store last night."

REFERENCES

Dickinson, D.K. 2011. "Teachers' Language Practices and Academic Outcomes of Preschool Children." *Science* 333 (6045): 964–67.

Dickinson, D.K., & M.V. Porche. 2011. "Relation Between Language Experiences in Preschool Classrooms and Children's Kindergarten and Fourth-Grade Language and Reading Abilities." *Child Development* 82 (3): 870–86. http://onlinelibrary.wiley.com/doi/10.1111/j.1467-8624.2011.01576.x/pdf.

Wetzel, J. 2011. "'Robust' Link Between Preschool, Language and Literacy." Vanderbilt University: Research News at Vanderbilt. http://news.vanderbilt.edu/2011/08/preschool-language-literacy.

Where would you be without words? You couldn't say "Hello" or "Nice to see you." Or get what you need. Or thank someone for a kind gesture. Your feelings would stay buried inside. You'd stay lost if you couldn't ask for directions. And when the day ends, how would you say goodnight? Whether spoken or written or signed, the words that you understand when you hear or see them (your *receptive* vocabulary) and the words you use to communicate (your *expressive* vocabulary) allow you to function every day.

Tips for Adding Rich Vocabulary to Your Interactions With Children

Create and post lists of interesting words. Write and display lists of attention-grabbing words in every learning center.

Read aloud. Look for picture books with challenging, colorful words so children can build their vocabularies.

Grow your own vocabulary. Do crossword, find-a-word, and jumble puzzles; brainstorm words with colleagues in staff meetings; and learn a few words in children's home languages.

Give hints. To help children understand unfamiliar words, use visual clues, gestures, and facial expressions.

Converse, converse, converse! A culture of conversation will go a long way toward building children's vocabularies. Use the word *conversation* with children. Encourage children's conversations with each other; for example, tell them, "While we have snack, you can have a conversation with the person next to you." Post questions and comments to serve as conversation starters.

Create a world of words. Sing songs and recite poems with children. Talk about new words as they come up in conversations and books. Make "word-for-the-day" part of the daily routine. Post a sign in the library area: "Interesting Words We've Found in Books." Add the job of "vocabulary builder" to the roster of classroom jobs. When children ask about a particular word, build on their curiosity: "You're curious about that word, aren't you? I'll read that part again. Do you have any guesses about what it means?"

Adapted from A.L. Dombro, J. Jablon, & C. Stetson, *Powerful Interactions: How to Connect With Children to Extend Their Learning* (Washington, DC: NAEYC, 2011), 113–16.

Recommendations for enhancing the language and literacy environment need to be extended to children who speak different languages. Staff and volunteers who speak other languages need to use the same strategies in those languages. The quality, richness, and stimulation provided by bilingual helpers should match the sophisticated vocabulary and extended conversations used with English-speaking children.

Co-Creating Scripts With Young Children to Help Them Feel Better

Carol Garboden Murray

> Charlie lost his glove.
> Charlie says, "I Love my glove. I WANT my glove."
>
> If you find it, charlie says: "Give it to me!"
>
> Thank you.

If you've ever kept a journal, you know that expressing your feelings in writing can be therapeutic. Young children can also experience self-expression, emotional validation, and relief through writing. When children see their words printed and listen as their teacher reads them aloud, their language and emotions have power and meaning.

Preschool teachers have long known the benefits of taking child dictations. Co-creating scripts is a similar process, but the teacher takes a more active role. The teacher offers to help the child solve a problem by writing down his words and ideas. A teacher asking a child who seems sad if he would like to write a letter to his mom (whom he is really missing) is a perfect example of co-creating a script.

Charlie's Red Glove

Charlie, a bright and sensitive preschooler, had difficulty with transitions and often found the busy classroom overwhelming. He sought quiet places and sedentary play.

Today Charlie was sobbing; he had lost one of his red gloves. All of the teachers tried to console and comfort him. They helped him search for the missing glove and suggested that perhaps his mom had accidentally taken it with her. Nothing seemed to help. Charlie had one glove on, and the other was missing. He refused to borrow from the mitten basket. He wouldn't budge from his cubby.

I sat down on the floor next to Charlie's cubby with my clipboard, trying to decide how I might help. A few days earlier, when he'd had a hard time separating from his mom, we had co-created a letter. With each sentence dictated and reread, I could see him released from his stress. When we had finished the letter, Charlie had folded it up in the crumpled way 3-year-olds fold paper, stuffed it in his backpack, and moved into the classroom to play.

On this day I talked with Charlie again. I asked simple yes and no questions that I felt would validate his longing for his missing glove.

"Charlie, was your glove red?"

Charlie nodded.

"Here is a red marker. Charlie, I want to draw a picture of your red glove so that I can remember what it looks like."

Another nod.

"Can I see your other glove? I can trace it and make a picture of your missing glove."

As I carefully traced the glove, Charlie stopped crying and watched me color in each finger with the red marker. We sat quietly together while I worked on my clipboard, which was tipped in Charlie's direction. Although I colored in silence, I tried to involve Charlie by moving the marker slowly and watching his response. The coloring itself gave us a peaceful shared moment and a certain distraction from the previous stress.

Next, I said, "I have an idea. Sometimes when people lose something, they make a sign for everyone to read. Would you like to help me write a sign about your glove? We can hang it on the door. If someone finds the glove, they will know it is yours."

Charlie looked at me and said, "Yes!"

After writing the note with Charlie, I read his words back to him several times. When he agreed that the sign was done, we taped it to the classroom door. On page 78, you can see the sign we co-created and read Charlie's exact words in quotation marks.

Charlie ran outside gloveless to enjoy the last 10 minutes of playtime. A few days later we all enjoyed a giant class cheer when the missing glove turned up in a playmate's backpack.

This life experience let Charlie know that he could cope with his own difficult emotions. Through an emergent literacy activity as simple as making a sign, Charlie had a real-life lesson that supported his emotional life, contributed to a responsive and caring classroom, and demonstrated the power of language.

Two Strategies in One

What could be more meaningful and tangible in the life of a young child than writing about an emotionally charged event? Co-creating scripts with children is a dual-purpose strategy. It responds to children's strong emotions while also creating a literacy experience. Experiencing and expressing strong emotions is new and sometimes frightening for children. When adults respond with care, children can develop healthy attitudes about themselves as individuals and as members of a group.

Supporting Dual Language Learners

Even if you don't speak a child's language, you can still support his or her self-expression. Try taking dictation phonetically—listen carefully and capture the sounds of the child's words. In the moment, you will be showing the child that his or her words are just as important as every other child's. A parent or volunteer can help you translate later.

Taking the time to learn a few key phrases in each child's language will also help you write down children's words. Ask parents to help you learn to say "Tell me more" or "What do you want me to write?" Then work collaboratively with each child to build that bridge of communication.

Grab your clipboard and stay close to the child. The first few times it may feel a bit awkward and unnatural for you and the child. Comfort and ease will grow as you build a reflective community that solves problems by writing them down.

Ask a question or use a simple phrase or other prompt if the child needs support verbalizing.

"Maybe we could make a list of things you are worried about."

"I wonder what you want to say next."

Act as a coach, but let the child talk. Ask open-ended questions, and invite the child to respond. Don't speak for the child or assume you know what the child is thinking or feeling. The adult's role is to write the child's words exactly as he or she speaks them, while acting as a coach by making suggestions. ("Do you want to write a letter/make a sign/develop a list?")

Read the sentences or words back to the child several times. Rereading the child's words and phrases is an effective validation tool. This is also an important step in helping the child slow down, breathe, listen, and reflect.

Create a "Let's write that down" atmosphere in your classroom. When a child makes a suggestion about which story he wants to read at group time, you can say, "That's a great idea. Let me write that down so I remember it." When a child is crying because she didn't get a turn with the magnets at the science center, you can say, "I'm going to write a note that Amanda wants a turn with the magnets."

Tips for Talking With Children

Judy Jablon, With Charlotte Stetson

See how much happens in this short conversation:

Lucy: I helped Mommy make muffins. We had 'gredients.

Ms. Allan: What ingredients did you use?

Lucy: I poured the flour and stirred the egg. Know what? The flour got on me and the floor.

Ms. Allan: Then what happened?

Lucy: We put blueberries in the bowl, 100 cups!

Ms. Allan: That's a lot of blueberries.

Lucy: I put them in all by myself.

In less than a minute, this teacher learns that 4-year-old Lucy feels confident and proud about helping her mother bake, is working on number concepts and measurement, and is eager to talk and share stories. In response, Lucy's teacher plans a cooking activity, adds a new counting game to the math area, and writes a note to herself to read *Blueberries for Sal*, by Robert McCloskey, with Lucy.

Through this brief chat, Lucy is learning new words and how to form sentences. She is learning how to listen. These are skills Lucy—and all children—will build on as they learn to read and write. Here are 10 tips for having good conversations with young children.

1. **Make sure both people get a turn.** A conversation doesn't have to be long, but it does have to involve taking turns talking and listening. Aim to switch speakers at least five times.

2. **Use facial expressions and comments.** They show you are listening and interested in the child's ideas and comments. Nod your head, smile, or laugh. Add "Mm-hmm," "Really?" or "Tell me more about that."

3. **Pause after you say something.** This gives children time to think and focus on their ideas.

4. **Describe what you see children doing.** Young children often talk as they draw, paint, and build. Say, "I notice you are using a lot of orange paint. What made you decide to use that color?" "What does your painting remind you of?"

5. **Ask children to tell you their stories.** When Liana shows you her new shoes, you could say, "I see you have new red shoes. Tell me about your trip to the store to buy them."

6. **Talk about books.** After reading time, ask children "What did you like about that story? What didn't you like?" "Who does that character remind you of? Why?" "There was one part that made us all laugh. What else did you think was funny in the story?"

7. **Invite children to teach you how to do something.** Children may simply demonstrate, but as they do, you can carry on the conversation. "Tell me how you draw houses. I see you are making some straight lines. Oh, and squares for the windows."

8. **Ask open-ended questions.** Children can then come up with a variety of answers. For example, ask, "What are some things you notice about the guinea pig?" Avoid questions with one-word answers: "What color is that?" "How many peas do you have on your plate?" Questions like these stop the conversation.

9. **Encourage self-expression.** Some children express their opinions freely; others need to be asked their views. "What do you think about this artwork?" "Why do/don't you like today's snack?"

10. **Connect the conversation to the child.** You can refer to a child's home life, previous events, or other things you've talked about. On Monday morning, say to Marc, "You were excited about going to your grandpa's birthday party this weekend. Tell me all about it."

Poetry Books for Preschoolers

Susan Friedman

From silly verses to those that describe emotions, preschoolers enjoy listening to many kinds of poems. And as they listen, they hear rhythms, sounds, and language patterns important for literacy development. Try these books and activities to bring poetry to your classroom and to encourage the poet within each child. All are great additions to a preschool library.

Here's a Little Poem: A Very First Book of Poetry, collected by Jane Yolen and Andrew Fuseks Peters. Illus. by Polly Dunbar. 2007. Candlewick.

Selected with young children in mind, each poem relates to their day-to-day lives. The book includes many different kinds of short poems, from the silly "Dressing Too Quickly" to "The No-No Bird" about a child's tantrum. Children can explore works by a variety of poets, including Jack Prelutsky, Margaret Wise Brown, and Langston Hughes.

In Aunt Giraffe's Green Garden, by Jack Prelutsky. Illus. by Petra Mathers. 2007. Greenwillow.

Each of the 28 poems tells a unique rhyming story. Many mention specific US locations. The humor, word choices, and topics are all perfect for preschoolers.

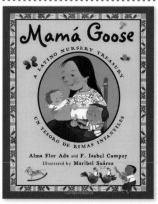

Mama Goose: A Latino Nursery Treasury, by Alma Flor Ada and F. Isabel Campoy. Illus. by Maribel Suarez. 2006. Disney-Hyperion.

This book features 68 poems, nursery rhymes, riddles, songs, puppet plays, and more from Latino cultures. Read selected poems in both Spanish and English. The illustrations are bright, fun, and reflect the fun quality of the poems. This book is a charming celebration of two cultures and Latin folklore.

Encourage rhyming. Read a short rhyming poem. As you reread it, stop before reading the second rhyming word. Invite children to finish the rhyme themselves. It's OK if children suggest words that don't make sense or don't rhyme.

Learn new words. Read a poem that introduces a new word or uses a familiar word in an unusual way. Ask, "Does anyone know what this word means? What other words could you use instead?" As the class brainstorms words together, make a list to read back to the group.

Explore emotions. Many poems describe emotions or moods children have experienced. After reading such a poem, ask, "What do you think the poet was feeling? Have you ever felt like that?"

Develop observational skills. After reading a poem inspired by nature, go outdoors. Take along magnifying glasses, paper and crayons, or digital cameras to help children with their observations. Later, ask if anyone wants to write a poem about what they saw or heard.

Create a poem. For inspiration, discuss the children's interests, feelings, or families, or take children outside to observe. Write down children's words as they say them. Provide art materials so children can illustrate their work. Remember, poems do not have to rhyme and can be about anything at all.

Involve families. Send home a poem for families to read together. Or invite families to a class poetry reading. They can read aloud the poems the children wrote and share their own favorite poems.

In the Wild, by David Elliott. Illus. by Holly Meade. 2013. Candlewick Press.

Each poem in this book focuses on a different wild animal, from the arctic polar bear to a desert giraffe. This book offers a great introduction to a study about wild animals or poetry.

Using Read-Alouds to Explore
Tender Topics

Sue Mankiw and Janis Strasser

O n any day, in any preschool classroom, you might witness the following scenes:

- Lamar, whose parents have just separated, is crying because he left his mittens at his dad's house over the weekend.
- Mario and Alyssa are arguing. He says, "There is no such thing as two mommies. My mommy and meemaw told me that."
- Sarah asks Jorge why his brother makes weird noises and walks and talks funny.
- James says he's afraid of the new boy because his skin is brown.

These children are talking about tender topics such as divorce, family composition, having a sibling with autism, and ethnic diversity. Some preschool teachers, in some situations, can find it difficult to discuss topics such as these with children. It helps to view tender topics not as problems, but as typical events and situations in the everyday lives of children and families.

Explore Stories Thoughtfully

Storybooks allow children to meet characters who are similar to them. Bibliotherapy is the art of using storybooks to help individual or small groups of children understand specific difficult experiences (Thibault 2004). Bibliotherapy is a developmentally appropriate way for teachers to help children think about the meaning of the story, characters, setting, and illustrations. With a teacher's guidance, children can relate to the events and characters in the story and better understand their own experiences and those of classmates, family members, and other people.

Before addressing any tender topic, be sure to consider the children's developmental levels, individual needs, and families. Ask and answer questions, and listen to children's responses. After reading a book on a tender topic, discuss the meaning of the text and illustrations. Invite critical conversations, which probe children's thinking. Ask children to share their ideas. You will begin to understand their values, learn about their experiences, and clarify misunderstandings about the topic. For example, some children might assume that all families have a mother and a father, or they might believe that people who use wheelchairs are helpless.

Here are some questions to consider:

- Should you discuss this tender topic with a child or should you first discuss it with a parent or guardian?
- Is the book appropriate for all the children in the class or is it especially suited to one particular child?
- Should you read the book to the whole group, a small group, or just one child?
- What do you know about how the topic affects the children in the group?
- How will you inform and include families in the curriculum?

Evaluate the Content of Books

Before reading about tender topics with preschoolers, it's important to read the books and consider whether they are a good fit for the individual or the group. Here are some questions that can help you evaluate a book:

- Do the illustrations or storylines depict stereotypes, such as people in particular ethnic groups living in poverty or characters with disabilities who succeed only with the help of characters without disabilities?
- Does the author have personal experience with this topic? Research the author's website or examine the dust jacket or the book's last pages, where authors typically share their connections to the story.
- Are problems solved realistically? Does the story allow multiple solutions? Can children figure out how they would approach the problem?
- Is the writing style likely to encourage discussion?
- How does the author describe the characters? For example, are people with special needs pitied and described as helpless?
- Is the story developmentally appropriate and interesting? Are the illustrations eye-catching? Is the text written for young children?

Be sure to read aloud books about tender topics daily. These topics appear in the everyday lives of children, so they need to be included and valued in the everyday curriculum.

Storybook Suggestions

For the children who raised the tender topics mentioned above, here are storybook suggestions.

Divorce

***The Family Book* (2003), by Todd Parr; *Mama and Daddy Bear's Divorce* (1998), by Cornelia Maude Spelman, illus. by Kathy Parkinson.**

When Ms. Denny reads *The Family Book* to 4-year-old Lamar, it leads to a discussion about different kinds of families. She asks Lamar to bring photos of his mom and dad to hang in his cubby. He can visit there when he misses them. Ms. Denny lends two copies of *Mama and Daddy Bear's Divorce* to Lamar's mother and father. She explains to each parent how reading the story with Lamar will help him ask questions about their divorce. Having answers to his questions might calm his anxiety about living in two homes.

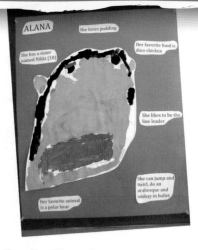

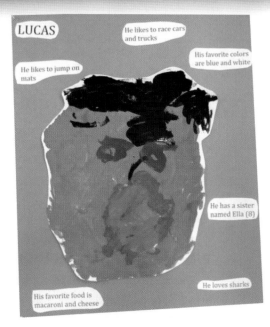

Family Diversity

The Family Book (2003), by Todd Parr.

At circle time, Mr. Thompson reads *The Family Book*, which mentions all kinds of families, including same-sex parents. At the end of the day he sends home a note asking families to send in photographs of the people in their family. At circle time the children use the photos to introduce their families to each other. This leads to many engaging conversations about different kinds of families.

Disabilities

***Ian's Walk: A Story About Autism* (1998), by Laurie Lears, illus. by Karen Ritz.**

When Ms. Langford takes Sarah and Jorge for a walk in the neighborhood they talk about Jorge's brother, Leon. How would Leon react if he heard that dog barking? What are his favorite things to do? Later, they read *Ian's Walk*, a story about a girl whose brother gets lost on a walk. Finding him means figuring out what he likes and how he explores his environment. Ian has autism, and Jorge can safely talk to Ms. Langford and Sarah about what that means for his brother Leon.

Race

***The Skin You Live In* (2005), by Michael Tyler, illus. by David Lee Csicsko; *The Colors of Us* (1999), by Karen Katz.**

By age 3 children begin to notice physical differences in people. Some children are both curious about and afraid of differences they notice. Hearing James' fear, Mr. Conway realizes he needs to plan a project where the children can talk about diversity. In small groups, Mr. Conway reads stories about skin color. Since James' comment was about skin color, Mr. Conway does not view it as racist, but rather as a topic to explore. After reading *The Skin You Live In* and *The Colors of Us*, children explore multicultural paints. Working in pairs, children mix paint to match their skin color. They use descriptive language to name their paint color, and they create self-portraits.

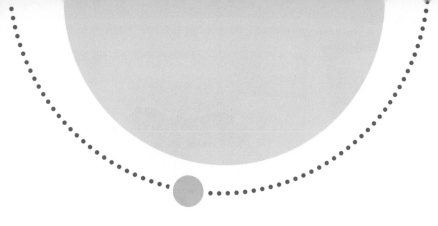

Where Can Teachers Begin?

Read a book about tender topics to yourself. Think about your experiences, feelings, and biases. Are you comfortable reading this story to young children? If not, read it to a friend or another teacher. By starting conversations with colleagues, you may gain new perspectives and confidence in approaching the topic. Including all aspects of children's lives and families in the curriculum sends important messages about caring and respect.

Think about how you can support children's understanding of tender topics. Read two or more books about the same tender topic. The stories will become an important resource for addressing children's misunderstandings and helping them talk.

Families can be a great resource for discussing these topics and answering children's questions. A family member who feels comfortable with this might visit the class to share information or answer children's questions. To prepare children for the visit, read and discuss stories about the tender topic.

Be Prepared to Address Misunderstandings

At circle time one day, Ms. Brown reads these lines in *Kathy's Hats: A Story of Hope*, by Trudy Krisher: "One year something happened that doesn't happen to many children, but it happened to me. That something was a very serious disease. Its name was cancer."

Ms. Brown asks, "Does anyone know what cancer is?" Becky answers, "Cancer is when something falls off your body." As the story proceeds, Kathy loses her hair after having chemotherapy. Becky says, "I told you. Her hair is falling off. When my grandma had cancer, her leg fell off." From her family's experience, Becky has some understanding of cancer. Ms. Brown accepts the answer and later that day speaks to Becky's mother about her child's responses. Until now, Ms. Brown was unaware of this event in Becky's family.

As teachers invite conversations about tender topics, children might raise concerns that don't initially make sense from an adult point of view. Like Ms. Brown, teachers need to accept children's answers and listen carefully to understand how children use real-life experiences to build knowledge about the world.

Hearing children's experiences and ideas are the first steps toward addressing misunderstandings. When approaching tender topics with children and families, listen to and respect each other. Address misunderstandings with simple, honest explanations. Always include families.

Conclusion

Reading books and talking about sensitive topics requires courage and honesty. Explore these topics as children raise them and as part of day-to-day life in your early childhood setting. Offer simple, realistic explanations. Listen and respect each others' feelings. Teachers don't need to have all the answers. Starting the conversation is most important.

REFERENCE

Thibault, M. 2004. "Children's Literature Promotes Understanding." *Learn NC.* www.learnnc.org/lp/pages/635.

Supporting Dual Language Learners

Discussing tender topics is not easy for anyone. Language differences can lead to misunderstandings that make these topics even more worrisome for children who are dual language learners (DLLs). It is important to have good quality books on needed topics available in children's home languages so they can fully understand what's happening. When tender topics come up, it is a good idea to let families of DLLs know so they are prepared to explain the issue and offer support to their child.

Literacy Learning Center Checklist

Laura J. Colker

 ou can complete this checklist for the literacy center in your classroom on your own or with a teaching colleague. When you are finished, review the items you rated as "rarely" and create an action plan to help change the rating to "sometimes or "regularly."

	Regularly	Sometimes	Rarely
1. Children choose to play in the literacy center every day.	○	○	○
2. Children know and follow the rules for using and returning books and other materials.	○	○	○
3. The center is located away from louder areas, such as the music and movement center.	○	○	○
4. Materials and books are stored on shelves or in labeled containers within children's reach.	○	○	○
5. There are books about reading and literacy.	○	○	○
6. Children can use bookmarks to mark pages where they left off and return to books later.	○	○	○
7. Children have fun and express pleasure in playing in the literacy center.	○	○	○
8. While playing in the literacy center, children can express thoughts and feelings and build skills in all domains.	○	○	○
9. The literacy center has			
• Materials used to draw, scribble, and write	○	○	○
• Stories on tape or CD	○	○	○
• A variety of fiction and nonfiction books and other text	○	○	○
• Books in English and in children's home languages	○	○	○
• Materials and props children use for follow-up activities	○	○	○
10. Teachers extend children's play by			
• Asking questions	○	○	○
• Offering ideas	○	○	○
• Commenting on their work	○	○	○
• Providing new materials that offer different experiences	○	○	○

Credits

"A Trip to the Book Hospital" is adapted from *Learning to Read and Write: Developmentally Appropriate Practices for Young Children*, by Susan B. Neuman, Carol Copple, and Sue Bredekamp, page 37.

"Conversations With Preschoolers: Learning to Give and Take" is adapted from *The Intentional Teacher: Choosing the Best Strategies for Young Children's Learning, Revised Edition*, pages 104–6.

The following are selections published previously in *Teaching Young Children* and the issues in which they appeared:

"Reading, Writing, and Talking: Strategies for Preschool Classrooms," February 2009
"Sagacious, Sophisticated, and Sedulous: Introducing 50-Cent Words to Preschoolers," April 2013
"Supporting Writing in Preschool," May 2008
"Literacy Learning Center," December 2009
"A Place for Publishing," October 2011
"Children's Book Authors on Reading," December 2010

"Sharing Time: So Much More Than Show and Tell," June 2009

"Literacy Begins With Language Skills," April 2010

"A Trip to the Book Hospital," February 2009

"Real-Life Reasons to Write," June 2009

"Get to Know the New Children's Librarian," December 2013

"Writing Poetry With Preschoolers," December 2013

"Using Multiple Texts to Guide Children's Learning," February 2013

"Resources for Identifying Wonderful Children's Books," October 2011

"Magazines for Preschoolers," June 2009

"Nontraditional Books to Engage Emergent Readers," December 2011

"Talk Now, Read Later," December 2011

"Co-Creating Scripts With Young Children to Help Them Feel Better," December 2008

 "Tips for Talking With Children," November 2007

"Poetry Books for Preschoolers," October 2008

"Tender Topics: Using Read Alouds to Explore Sensitive Issues," June 2013

The following are adaptations of articles published previously in *Young Children* and the issues in which they appeared:

"Tender Topics: Using Read Alouds to Explore Sensitive Issues," March 2013

"Sagacious, Sophisticated, and Sedulous: Introducing 50-Cent Words to Preschoolers," November 2012

"Rap and Young Children: Encouraging Preschoolers' Emergent Literacy," July 2014

"Helping Preschoolers Prepare for Writing: Developing Fine Motor Skills," September 2011

About the Authors

Lauren Baker is an assistant editor at NAEYC. She writes and edits for the magazine *Teaching Young Children*.

Michelle Bloom, MEd, is a certified pre-K through grade 6 teacher. She has spent most of her career teaching in early childhood and primary grade classrooms.

Cen Campbell is a children's librarian who lives in Mountain View, California. She is the founder of LittleeLit.com.

Carolyn Carlson, PhD, lives in Topeka, Kansas. She works at Washburn University as an associate professor of literacy education.

Pamela Hobart Carter lives in Seattle, Washington. She worked at New Discovery School for the last 16 years of

her 30 in the classroom and has just taken up writing, full-time. She continues to teach poetry with preschoolers.

James F. Christie lives in Phoenix, Arizona. He is professor emeritus in the T. Denny Sanford School of Social and Family Dynamics at Arizona State University.

Kathleen Chvostal-Schmidt, MA, resides in Hammond, Indiana, where she lives with her husband. She has been employed by the SPEED Special Education Cooperative for 17 years. She works in the Birth to 3 at-risk program for SPEED's Family Enrichment Program.

Laura J. Colker, EdD, of Washington, DC, is president of L.J. Colker & Associates. In addition to being a contributing editor of *Teaching Young Children*, she has authored more than 100 publications and instructional guides, including co-authorship of *The Creative Curriculum for Preschool*.

Molly F. Collins lives in Nashville, Tennessee. She works at in the Department of Teaching and Learning at Vanderbilt University as a lecturer.

Linda Dauksas, EdD, lives in Burr Ridge, Illinois. She is an associate professor and director of early childhood education at Elmhurst College. Before joining the faculty, Dr. Dauksas dedicated 30 years to teaching and leading programs for young children and families.

Meghan Dombrink-Green received her master's degree from Johns Hopkins University and served as a Fulbright English Teaching Assistant to Cyprus. She is an associate editor at NAEYC, working primarily on *Teaching Young Children*.

Ann S. Epstein is the senior director of curriculum development at HighScope Educational Research Foundation in Ypsilanti, Michigan. She is the author of *The Intentional Teacher: Choosing the Best Strategies for Young Children's Learning, Revised Edition.*

Callie Fortenberry, EdD, lives in Mt. Pleasant, Texas. She works at Texas A&M University-Texarkana as an associate professor of education and reading.

Susan Friedman is executive editor of digital content at NAEYC. She received her MEd from the Harvard Graduate School of Education. Formerly a preschool teacher, she has served as the editorial director for a number of educational websites.

Dr. J. Michelle Huffman lives in Mount Pleasant, Texas. She works for the Region 8 Education Service Center as the early childhood coordinator of curriculum and instruction.

Judy Jablon is an early childhood consultant and author and lives in South Orange, New Jersey. She supports educators, management teams, schools, and agencies through results-oriented professional development, coaching, consultation, facilitation, and project management.

Natalie Klein-Raymond is an editor and writer specializing in early childhood publications. She has worked for organizations such as NAEYC, Reading Is Fundamental, and Tools of the Mind.

Lisa Mufson Koeppel lives in Fair Lawn, New Jersey. She has been a preschool teacher in the Passaic Public School system for the past 10 years. Over the years, she has written about and presented on various topics in the field of early childhood education.

Derry Koralek, NAEYC's chief publishing officer, oversees the development of the association's award-winning, research-based periodicals and books. She has worked at NAEYC for nearly 14 years and is the founding editor in chief of *Teaching Young Children*.

Sue Mankiw is an associate professor of education at William Paterson University in Wayne, New Jersey, where she is the director of early childhood programs and teaches language arts and social studies methods courses.

Carol Garboden Murray is lives in New Paltz, New York. She is the director of the nursery school at Bard College.

Karen N. Nemeth is an author and consultant for www. LanguageCastle.com. She lives in Bucks County, Pennsylvania.

Evelyn A. O'Connor, PhD, is a professor and director of the literacy program in the Department of Curriculum and Instruction at Adelphi University, in New York. Her research focuses on emergent literacy, teacher professional development, and Reading Recovery.

Barbara Rando, MS, a retired classroom teacher, has been an adjunct professor at Adelphi University, New York University, and Queens College in New York.

Donald J. Richgels is Distinguished Research Professor Emeritus at Northern Illinois University.

Louis Mark Romei lives in North Brunswick, New Jersey. He works in the Office of Early Childhood for New Brunswick Public Schools as a master teacher.

Kathleen A. Roskos lives in Conneaut, Ohio. She works at John Carroll University as a professor of education.

Meagan K. Shedd lives in Plymouth, New Hampshire. She works at Plymouth State University as an assistant professor in the Early Childhood Studies Department.

Marie Sloane lives in Herndon, Virginia. She works as the director of education at Annandale Cooperative Preschool.

Charlotte Stetson lives in Hancock, Maine. Until her retirement in June, 2013, she was an independent early childhood consultant and author. She guided teachers in the areas of observation, assessment, curriculum, and teacher-child interactions and coauthored several publications, including *Powerful Interactions: How to Connect With Children to Extend Their Learning*.

Karen Steuerwalt, MA, is a lecturer and coordinator for the Elementary Education Master of Arts in Teaching program at Queens College, City University of New York. Karen has more than 20 years of experience in early childhood education. Her teaching focus is inquiry-based learning and connecting children to their natural world.

Janis Strasser lives in Ridgewood, New Jersey. She has been professor of early childhood education at William Paterson University for the past 16 years. Prior to that she taught preschool, kindergarten, first grade, and music and was an education coordinator for Head Start.

TEACHING YOUNG CHILDREN/PRESCHOOL

Much of the content in this book is adapted from *Teaching Young Children* (*TYC*), NAEYC's award-winning magazine, which celebrates and supports everyone who works with preschoolers. Each issue presents practical information through text, photographs, infographics, and illustrations. Short, research-based articles share ideas to use right away.

TYC is available as a member benefit or through subscription. If you like this book, go to www.naeyc.org to join NAEYC or become a *TYC* subscriber.